For Anna Bodo

BLOOMSBURY

Published by Rouleur Books
An imprint of Bloomsbury Publishing Plc
50 Bedford Square
London WC1B 3DP
www.bloomsbury.com

First edition 2012, Reprinted 2013

ISBN 978-1-4081-8166-9

A CIP catalogue record for this book is available from the British Library

Editor **Guy Andrews**
Sub editor **Claire Read**
Designer **Rob Johnston**
Editor of photography **Taz Darling**
Image retoucher **Linda Duong**
All photography © as indexed

Made from wood grown in managed, sustainable forests. It is natural, renewable and recyclable. The logging and manufacturing processes conform to the environmental regulations of the country of origin.

Printed and bound in China by C&C Offset Ltd

Rouleur Limited
1 Luke Street
London EC2A 4PX
www.rouleur.cc

Rouleur
Rouleur magazine is published eight times a year
ISSN 1752-962X

CONTENTS

INTRODUCTION

First a confession...

The reality is that I'd promised myself that I would never, under any circumstances, write a book about Fausto Coppi.

The reason, for what it's worth, is that there are just so very many of them, layer upon gormless layer. Every year Italy's bloated publishing industry belches out another load, each apparently revelatory, all apparently definitive. Very occasionally they are good, in the main they are categorically not, on occasion they are barely readable. More than 50 years on, the business of inducing Fausto Coppi – and the business of reinventing him – meanders on. The Coppi industry, it often seems, is immune to recession. As often as not it's also immune to good taste.

When you live in Coppi's Piedmont and have an interest in bike racing, the books come to assume pretty much the same status as bottles of the local plonk. Nobody ever seems to buy them and yet somehow they proliferate. I reckon I've two dozen or so on my bookshelves at any given time, not one of which I've actually paid for. Rather they seem simply to accumulate and ultimately to fester. From time to time I need the space and move a few on, and so the cycle continues...

Why then the change of heart? Moreover why, given that I maintain that I have precisely nothing new to say on the matter, have I been so presumptuous as to add to the heap? What could possibly be the point, and why might I commend to you yet another book about Fausto Coppi and post-war Italian cycling?

In July 2010 Giancarlo Astrua and Nino Defilippis, two former cyclists whom I'd known, passed away within a fortnight. Though very different, each was among the best of his generation and each a hero in Turin, my adopted home town. Astrua, a gutsy climber, had animated both the Tour and the Giro in the early 1950s. Though Coppi, Gino Bartali and Fiorenzo Magni won more and earned more, he was among the best of the rest; one of his country's favourite underdogs.

Defilippis was a fabulous, swashbuckling sprinter-roadman who had idolised Fausto as a boy. Coppi liked him a great deal and, as the sun set on his own career, Nino fleetingly usurped him at the top end of the sport here.

Since we lost Giancarlo and Nino, I've watched on as many more have breathed their last. A few – celebrated *gregari* like Ettore Milano and Stefano Gaggero – were honoured by the wider Italian cycling community. Most, however, had long since slipped beneath its collective radar. So prolific and so pervasive were Coppi and Bartali that the rivalries, successes and shortcomings of their contemporaries were largely overlooked. As such these men lived out their days anonymously, their cycling exploits obscured by the mists of time.

Each new year the great and the good of Italian cycling congregate at Castellania, a tiny hamlet in the Gavi hills. There they pay homage to Fausto and to Serse, the brother he lost in a racing accident in 1951. Every year, however, fewer of the people who rode with, for and against him are present. Within less than a decade those against whom he competed – those upon whom he had a direct, human effect – will be no more. With that in mind I began to visit them at home and to talk to them about their own lives as cyclists. I did so in the first instance with a view to simply preserving something of those lives; to gathering together some kind of oral history before it was too late. Having done so, and having been captivated by much of what they said, I decided that I owed it to them to share their memories. They may be the silent minority but their recollections, allied to the personal truths each of them jealously guards about Coppi, demand no less.

Our appreciation of and emotional attachment to champion cyclists isn't conditioned merely by what they do. Rather their greatness is to be found in the impact their exploits have on themselves, on those around them, and ultimately on the sport itself.

Il Campionissimo rode professionally for two decades either side of the war. His freakish talent spanned four generations over what remains, unquestionably, the golden age of cycling. Not only did he revolutionise much of its methodology, but his splenetic rivalry with Gino Bartali fired the collective imagination as never before. Since Fausto's demise their battle has come to assume all manner of (largely delusional) political and cultural symbolism. For all that the fact remains that it took place at a time of unprecedented social upheaval. As agrarian, Catholic Italy began to embrace urbanisation and modernity, the two cyclists were, thrillingly, hammer and tongs. Never before – and in truth never again – would racing be this good, or generate this much electricity.

All of the above, however, are matters of public record, and the last thing cycling needs is another distended 21st century Coppi biography. Rather I think it time for those who were actually there. Those who actually know...

Their careers, like those of Astrua and Defilippis, were simultaneously conditioned, undermined and dignified by Coppi's. In that respect it was they, the mortals whose toil his genius both ridiculed and sustained, who were most instrumental in creating his mythic status. They were the people closest to him, and they remain the people best qualified to preserve the tapestry upon which his legend was weaved. If in so doing they unpick some of the myths which have been grafted onto it over the decades, then so much the better.

As such this collection is produced in deference to the cyclists they were, and to the men they became. They weren't touched by greatness as was Fausto, but that's not to say that they gave any less of themselves. With any luck it will survive them and be read by the descendants they will never know, by the children of their grandchildren. For it is to them, fundamentally, that the book belongs.

If the first motivation for this 'work' is visceral, the second is rather more gratuitous. So popular was bike racing in post-war Italy that a small army of press photographers – some of them extraordinarily gifted – charted its every move. A handful of the images they created are iconic, ubiquitous even, but nowhere amid the Coppi liturgy has there been a legitimate, cohesive rendition of their work. The vast majority has remained unpublished, and that has always struck me as a travesty. This book is intended, probably conceitedly, to remedy that at least in part. Though I don't profess to be an expert, I would attest that many of the images contained herein are genuine works of art; genuine masterpieces of composition.

Gratuitous then, but no less compelling for it. Though most of the pictures here remain unsigned, the book is intended as homage to the likes of Luigi Bertazzini, Carlo Martini and the great Vito Liverani. For it was also they, and the journalists with whom they worked, who created the legend of Fausto Coppi for us.

I hope you enjoy the book as much as I enjoyed my small part in making it.

Herbie Sykes
Turin, July 2012

FAUSTIN

They'd met before the war, out dancing. He was the best dancer in the province. Poor Angiolina, they said, couldn't help but fall in love with him. He was a charmer all right. He'd chosen her. She'd been chosen.

They'd married in a hurry, no great to-do (and her the niece of a pastor...) and Maria had been born in October 1914. Two years later he went off to the front, but left her a little something behind, something to take care of. She was good and kind and she took care and she gave him a boy. Livio.

At Caporetto they slaughtered 11,000. He came home with a punctured leg, but he came home. He'd been chosen. She was beautiful and they called her Claudina. Her dad worked till dusk up there in the vineyards. He bought them all a house at the top.

It was the cyclist Girardengo who rebuilt Italy. He had a big villa in Novi Ligure, down in the valley. He was the *Campionissimo* and they came from all around. They came from Tortona and Alessandria because he belonged to them and they belonged to him. They came from Ovada and Gavi, from Voghera and Acqui. They came from Castellania.

She wanted to call the boy Angelo after her father but he said he wanted, just this once, to choose. He chose Fausto, his brother's name. He was born at harvest time; in September as the sun went down. His father took an evening off and they killed a pig. They drank wine.

Oh Angiolina, bell'Angiolina
Oh Angiolina, bell'Angiolina!
Innamorato io son di te,
Innamorato dall'altra sera,
Quando venni a ballar con me...

E tu portavi una gonna rossa,
E tu portavi una gonna rossa!
Ed il corpetto di seta blu,
E le scarpette con le rosette,
Fatte apposta per ben ballar...

We'll call him Angelo Fausto and that's that.
Goodnight my love.

He was a narrow boy who liked to be on his own. He and Livio knew where their grandfather kept the gun. They always cleaned it before they put it back so their grandfather wouldn't know. He doesn't say much, does he? He wanders off. His grandfather knew.

Livio took him to watch the bike races and he couldn't concentrate when he worked in the fields. He never gets anything done. They were secretly pleased when he told them. They all helped to kill the pig and the man said he'd ask around in Novi. Ettore gave him a job delivering meat to the rich folk. Look at his skinny little legs.

He called the bike 'Three Guns' and Ettore gave him five lire every Friday. He wasn't cut out for working in the fields anyway. He's not like the others, is he? His body didn't fit him. You'll outgrow your strength.

Uncle Fausto was best because he was a sailor and he told him the things he knew because he'd seen them. He said you can go anywhere you want and you should see him go and Guerra couldn't climb and Camusso was the Chamois of Cumiana and Linari was

the fastest and I met him. He did it at that new velodrome in Milan.
35,000 people. *35,000*. Imagine that, Faustin? It cost 570 lire but
he only had 60. What's going on in that head of yours, Faustin?
Leave him be.

At the weekend he'd get up early and disappear off. When he
got home he'd eat supper and disappear off. His little brother said
he could keep a secret. He followed them when they were out
training. He goes upstairs with the newspaper. It's not normal for
a boy his age.

Merlano said he need be there at 8.45am sharp and don't be late.
He set off one minute later every Monday because he didn't want to
be late. You'll be late, Faustin. He keeps photos under his pillow.

There's a letter for you, Faustin. It says it's from India, must be from
your uncle Fausto. It's got something in it.

It was a pearly grey Maino with drop handlebars, the most beautiful
thing he'd ever seen. He's in a world of his own.

Fausto told me he's been to Sanremo. Eat your supper, Serse.

He says he's been to Milan and he's been in the clouds.

ALDO RONCONI

**b Faenza, 1918
pro 1940–1952**

*Yellow jersey, stage winner and third overall, 1947 Tour de France
Italian national champion 1946
Stage winner 1946 Giro d'Italia*

I rode as a *stagiaire* for Legnano in the autumn of 1939, with a certain Fausto Coppi. They gave us both contracts and we were picked to ride the 1940 Giro as *gregari* for Bartali. What happened was that Bartali crashed on stage two, on the descent of the Scoffera. Pavesi, the *direttore sportivo*, said Coppi and Favalli needn't wait but that I had to stay behind with Gino. He was close to abandoning but I helped him get round. Coppi and Favalli took five minutes and Favalli won the stage, so Pavesi was right all along. He was full of bright ideas, Pavesi. He used a megaphone to bellow at us and then he made each of us wear a different coloured cap so as to distinguish between us. Mine was the black one and so, because my brother was a monk, a team-mate started calling me 'The Parson'. Somehow it stuck, and that was me for the rest of my career – The Parson.

On stage 11 Coppi did his big ride over Abetone to win the Giro. I was on his wheel when he went but there was no way I could stay with him. Neither could anybody else and I think that was the day everybody realised he was something special. Later that season I had my first big win, the Giro dell'Umbria. Next thing I knew, though, I was on a train headed for Montenegro. When I got there I still rode my bike but the uniform was a bit different. I was the battalion postman...

I was born in 1918, near Faenza. I finished primary school aged 11 to start work as a joiner. There was no way we could afford a bike but I was lucky because there was a mechanic living nearby and he gave me one for next to nothing. My parents weren't happy because they were convinced cycling was dangerous. Thinking about it today that seems odd. There were no virtually no cars on the roads because nobody could afford them.

My mum fell ill, and when she was on her deathbed she made me promise to stop riding for a year. I kept my word, but it was hard. I started racing in 1936 and the following year I started winning. I couldn't sprint but I was strong and I could climb, and that conditioned the way I raced. I was second in the Italian Amateur Championship and in 1938 I won a lot. When I won the Coppa Perugina they paid me 2,000 lire. To put that into context, my dad was a signalman earning 350 lire a month. With the money we had electricity installed at home and we had enough left over for winter mattresses and a sewing machine for my sister. My dad figured that maybe cycling wasn't such a bad idea after all.

I won the Italian Fascist Junior Championship as well, and two big Italo-German stage races. The first was Rome-Berlin, and then Milan-Munich. It was three stages: Milan-Trento, Trento-Innsbruck, and then Innsbruck-Munich. I won the final stage by 15 minutes. They selected me for the World Championships, but then the war started and it was cancelled...

In September 1943 they announced the armistice with the allies. I was shunted onto a goods wagon and that's where I spent the next ten days. The conditions were inhuman and we got off at a concentration camp in Linz. In retrospect though that journey saved my life; others were taken to Mauthausen, 25 kilometres away.

I got talking to a German engineer guy and told him about my having been a cyclist and having won Milan-Munich. He liked me and he liked cycling, and he had me posted to the camp farm. My life there was good. Amid the carnage of the camps I got all the bread and milk I needed. I was extremely lucky, the more so because the camp was on the right bank of the Danube. We were freed by the Americans, but had we been on the left bank we'd have been 'liberated' by the Russians. A lot of those who were on that side of the river never came home...

I got back to Faenza on 29 June, 1945 and the city had largely been destroyed. I had no money, no work and, worst of all, no bike. My brother gave me his life savings and said: "This is everything I have. Take it, and get yourself a bike." He knew that in giving me that money he was giving me back my life.

I went to see Bianchi first, but they weren't interested. They reckoned that, given my age and the fact that I'd been away for so long, I'd be better off doing something else. That was hard to swallow but I wasn't about to give up. I was lucky again, because my friend and training partner Vito Ortelli was the new star of Italian cycling. People thought he might challenge Coppi and Bartali at the Giro and he told Benotto he wanted me on the team.

Vito had the jersey for six days, but he lost it in the Dolomites. Then on stage 15 I had my day of grace. It was me, Coppi, Bartali and Ortelli, and I dropped them all at Passo Rolle. I rode into Trento alone, and my brother was there to see me cross the line. He hadn't

been given leave by the monastery, so he'd had to escape. It was he who'd believed in me after my years as a POW and the joy of him being present on my great day was immense. Bartali won the Giro but, notwithstanding that I was a *gregario* for Ortelli, I finished fifth. That secured my future as a cyclist but the best was still to come.

In August they had the Italian National Championships and the race they chose that year was the Tour of Tuscany. Bartali was the big favourite because he knew the roads inside out and because his form was so good. Anyway it was incredibly hot that day, and I tended to go well in the heat. Me and Ortelli broke away, but we were stopped at a closed level crossing. We had to wait six minutes and so the chase group caught us. The rule was that they had to make them wait but there were no timekeepers. Anyway Bini and Bartali were in the group, the two Tuscans, and so it suited everybody that it all came back together. When we set off again Bini attacked. While Ortelli and Bartali watched each other I tried to bridge across. By the time I reached him Bini was cooked, and I dropped him easily. I, a *Romagnolo*, won the *maglia tricolore* in Bartali's backyard...

Benotto doubled my salary and the following season they started suggesting I might have a chance at the Giro. I was fourth on GC after stage 15 but I got ill and had to abandon in the Dolomites.

After the Giro I got a call from a journalist from La Gazzetta dello Sport. Jacques Goddet had told him he wanted an Italian team at the Tour at any cost. Coppi and Bartali had apparently refused, because they were frightened of possible repercussions. The French hated us after what had happened during the war and as far as they were concerned all Italians were traitors and cowards.

The Tour was 4,642 kilometres over 21 stages – 800 kilometres longer than the Giro. We set off with no outright leader but we had some decent riders. On stage three we went from Brussels to Luxembourg, 314 kilometres with a 7.40am roll-out. We rode through mining villages full of migrant Italians. It was incredible, one of the most inspiring days of my life. I attacked 120 kilometres from the finish and won the stage. Afterwards I received sacks of letters from the miners, telling me how badly they were treated by the French and how much joy I'd brought them that day.

I got the *maillot jaune* on stage seven, but on the stage over the Galibier I got no help whatsoever. Two of the team, Brambilla and

Tacca, were naturalised French and it was clear they were scared of the ramifications of being seen to work as part of an Italian team. I kept the jersey but then lost it the following day because I punctured twice on Izoard and there was nobody to help. René Vietto won, and I lost seven minutes.

With three days to go Vietto was leading, Brambilla was second, and I was third at 3'55". Stage 19 was a lumpy 139 kilometre time trial in Brittany and the Italian press were convinced that Brambilla would get the jersey. They were right, but I also leapfrogged Vietto. Now I was 53 seconds behind Brambilla, with Jean Robic third at just under three minutes. Nothing happened the following day in Normandy and so we started the final stage as we were. It was 257 kilometres from Caen to Paris and we were hoping the French would call a truce, as per tradition. In the event we couldn't have been more wrong...

The break went, but after 80 kilometres Robic attacked on the Côte de Bonsecours. Brambilla cracked and I tried to get across, but this time I ran out of luck. The French and Belgians had Simplex groupsets but we had Campagnolo. We had to pedal backwards to change gear, and that was very difficult to do when you were climbing. It was slow and cumbersome and you always lost ground because of it. Fachleitner went across to Robic and by the time I'd got myself sorted out they had 300 metres; 500 at the bottom of the descent. Brambilla was stuffed but I still had a Belgian with me, Impanis. He was a really strong guy and I knew that if we worked we'd have a good chance to get across. I offered him 100,000 francs which, to be perfectly honest, I didn't even have myself. He said: "Look my friend, we've done a deal with the French. Sorry, but there's no way I can help you..."

Giordano Cottur tried to help, but then he punctured and I was left in no-man's land. Apparently Robic and Fachleitner were drafting cars as well, but the organisers put the red flag up to stop our DS going across to keep an eye on them. We lost 13 minutes and Robic won the Tour without ever having worn the yellow jersey. Fachleitner got second, which meant I was fourth overall, not even on the podium. They gave Impanis a special prize, 25,000 francs. I couldn't figure out why given that he hadn't done anything.

Anyway there were the usual insinuations, that the turncoat Italians had sold the Tour de France. Can you imagine that?

Selling the biggest race in the world? The race that guaranteed you fame and fortune for the rest of your life?

Later I was told that there no way I would ever have been allowed to win the Tour regardless. I'd been Italian Fascist Champion before the war, and had won those stage races between Italy and Germany. My winning would have been unthinkable for the French public, and for the Tour itself...

■

Writing for L'Équipe following the 1947 Tour, Jacques Goddet stated that: "Aldo Ronconi won the sympathy and admiration of the entire French public. A battle lost as his was is in fact a battle won. He was the most regular rider of this Tour de France, and its undoubted moral victor."

"On stage 11 Coppi did his big ride over Abetone to win the Giro. I was on his wheel when he went but there was no way I could stay with him. Neither could anybody else and I think that was the day everybody realised he was something special..."

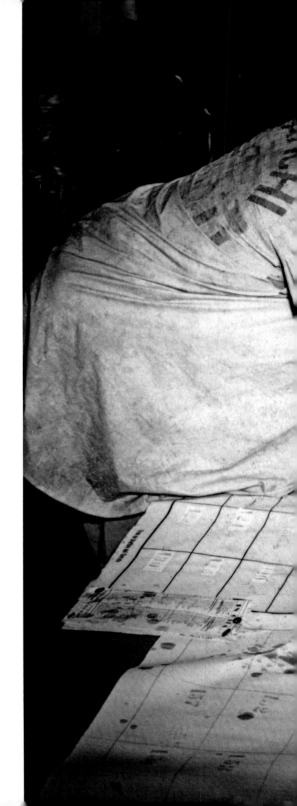

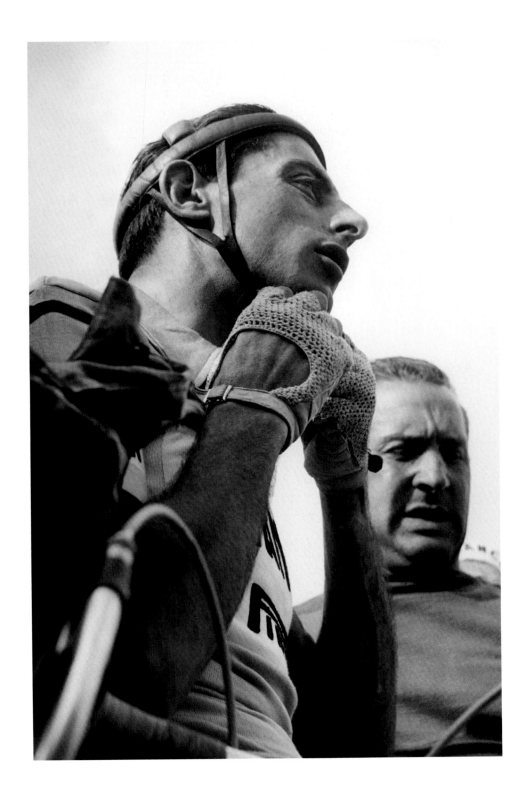

SERGIO MAGGINI

b Seano, 1920
pro 1945–1951

Stage winner 1949 Giro d'Italia
Winner Giro del Piemonte, Coppa Bernocchi, Milano-Torino
Third 1947 Milano-Sanremo

I was born near Florence in 1920 and I had a little brother, Luciano. When we were kids he was always pestering me to use my bike. They sent me to Greece during the war and when I got back he'd become the local champion. He'd 'borrowed' the bike and started racing. He'd apparently dropped it in the first race, picked himself up, caught the others and won by three minutes! Then he got sent off to war, and I got my bike back...

People tend to forget that everything was in ruins after the war. The train lines were broken and it wasn't as if you could just put the bike in the car like they do today. If there were races in Rome or in Milan you had to find a way to get there. You might get a lift in a truck from time to time but in the main you just rode your bike. From here to Rome or Milan you'd be talking more or less 350 kilometres. When you got there you'd find out what races there were and plan your time around them. That was how you made your money. You studied when and where to ride and you tried to figure out which races gave you the best odds.

While Luciano was away I won the biggest amateur race in Italy, the 1944 King's Cup. I got taken on by Benotto and I was a good professional. I couldn't sprint but I still won the Coppa Bernocchi and the Tour of Piedmont and meanwhile Luciano was winning in the amateurs. The publicity value of having two brothers was attractive to Benotto but most of all they were trying to break the Bianchi/Legnano duopoly. We already had a very good team but everyone could see that my brother was going to be a star in his own right. They took him on and in October our dream came true; we rode Lombardy together as professional cyclists.

When we came back the following spring we did the Tour of Sardinia, which was four stages, then Milan-Turin. That was the curtain raiser for Sanremo but it was very different back then. When I won it I only had about 800 kilometres in my legs. Sanremo was 19 March, St Joseph's Day. The 1947 race was one of the worst days I ever had on a bike, and one of the best. It was already snowing when we set off and we spent eight and a half hours battling against rain, hailstones and freezing cold. There was a raging headwind all the way along the coast and I think over 100 abandoned. Coppi looked terrible that day. He was already suffering from conjunctivitis and when we got over the Turchino he just carried on, went home. Bartali won, Cecchi was second and me and my brother got third and fourth. Eight Tuscans in the top ten at the *Primavera*; can you imagine that?

Luciano was five years younger than me. I was strong, but he was quicker and so for every race I won he'd win three or four. He wasn't as good as Coppi and Bartali though was right up there with the likes of Bevilacqua and Leoni. He was unknown out of Italy, but the world was much smaller back then.

We hardly ever rode outside of Italy. We never got to ride the Tour and that was always the big regret because of the prestige and the money you could earn. We did Roubaix and it probably suited us because we were strong. The problem was that we didn't really understand how to ride it.

Luciano was fourth at the World Championships at Valkenburg in 1948 and he rode a great race. Nobody took a blind bit of notice though. As usual they were too busy focusing on Coppi and Bartali. Everybody spent so much time discussing what they hadn't done that they barely noticed what he had...

——

Though the war cost Sergio Maggini a large part of his cycling career he still rode professionally for seven years. He was exceptionally strong but his inability to sprint cost him dear – while he collected a string of podium places, he won just nine times. His younger brother Luciano, whom he survived, was one of the very best riders in Italy.

"People tend to forget that everything was in ruins after the war. The train lines were broken and it wasn't as if you could just put the bike in the car like they do today. If there were races in Rome or in Milan you had to find a way to get there..."

VITO ORTELLI

b Faenza, 1921
pro 1940–1952

Italian pursuit champion 1945
Italian road champion 1948
Pink jersey and third overall 1946 Giro d'Italia
Pink jersey and fourth overall 1948 Giro d'Italia

A guy came to see me a few years ago and he was researching a book about Coppi and Eddy Merckx. He was trying to determine who was the better cyclist, which of course is something you can't objectively do. At the end he concluded that if they raced ten times over all different disciplines, distances and terrains, Merckx would probably have won seven and Coppi three. He also concluded that the three Coppi won would have been inspirational, romantic and beautiful. All the things Merckx wasn't...

I had a lot of time for Coppi because he was serious, honest and professional. He took pride in what he did and he was totally concentrated on it. We had our ups and downs but we respected one another and he never lied to me. We didn't speak for 18 months once but that was a stupid misunderstanding. In many ways it was typical of cycling back then, because it was a jungle.

It happened at the National Pursuit Championship in 1945. The championship was at the velodrome in Turin. I'd travelled overnight from Faenza, 400 kilometres on a slaughterman's wagon full of stinking pigs. The truck punctured in the small hours and they didn't have a spare so they had to wait for someone to turn up with one. One way or another I barely got any sleep and by the time they dropped me off outside Turin I was panicking I wouldn't make it in time. I rode the last 20 kilometres to the velodrome and just about managed to sign on.

The problem was that only seven signed up to ride the pursuit and so there was no way they could run a quarter final. Instead of simply giving somebody a bye, they offered to pay three of us 12,000 lire each. That was fine but most of the others were from nearby. I'd travelled much further and so I needed to eat, find a hotel and get the train back. It was much more expensive for me and so I said I wanted 15,000 to pay for it all. They refused and in the end they didn't get enough takers anyway. Leoni was given a bye instead and I won my quarter final. I drew Coppi in the semi...

Unbeknownst to me Coppi's masseur Biagio Cavanna went up to Graglia, the DS of my Benotto team. He said: "Given that Ortelli was happy to scratch for 15,000, we'll give him 20,000 to give Fausto an easy ride." They figured that I was so exhausted from the journey that Coppi would probably beat me anyway, but that he would have to go hard to do so. He'd therefore be exhausted for the final and Leoni, the other finalist, was not only very good but also very fresh. Graglia accepted their offer but he too assumed Coppi would win. Therefore he gambled on not telling me about it because that way he could keep all the money himself. I rode to win, obviously, and Coppi was off the pace straight away. He thought I'd slacken off and allow him to beat me but I won by four metres. Then I broke the track record to beat Leoni in the final. Benotto made a big deal out of it because they were from Turin and Coppi had just signed for Bianchi.

Coppi and I had always got on well. For some reason, though, he ignored me when I waved to him afterwards. That wasn't like him at all but I just assumed he was upset because he wasn't used to losing pursuits. Someone said he had been really angry after the race but I didn't think much of it; nobody likes getting beaten, especially when there's a *maglia tricolore* at stake.

I beat him again a few weeks later at Piacenza. After the race the Bianchi car broke down and he sent somebody to ask me to give him a lift to the station. I had no problem with that but it was strange because he didn't ask me himself and then he could barely bring himself to look at me. He barely said a word again and I thought he had a cheek asking me for a lift and then ignoring me...

I won a lot and before the 1946 season there was the usual debate about who would win what. Coppi was the favourite for the Giro, without question, but some said I would challenge him. I was the 'third man', though with the results I'd had during the war years a lot of people said I would take over from Bartali. I got ill just before the Giro though and I was a couple of kilogrammes underweight at the start.

Coppi still wasn't speaking to me, and on the second stage to Genoa, Bartali and I dropped him on the Caprile. I could have ridden away from Bartali on the flat but he offered me the stage and it made sense for us to ride through and off all the way to Genoa. Then, typical him, he attacked me as we entered the stadium and won. I confronted him and he just said: "Yes, but Martano did the same to me two years ago!" That was an unbelievably stupid thing to have said but it was classic Bartali. Anyway I won in Chieti and had the jersey for a week but then I punctured on the descent of the Falzarego and lost a load of time. The illness caught up with me and I finished third overall.

The following year at the Giro I was fourth but I was never really in contention. Coppi and Bartali were very close on GC and so Servadei, a friend of mine who was a *gregario* for Coppi, came to see me. We agreed a deal for me to help him but then he came back saying Coppi was having nothing to do with me after what had happened in Turin. He said: "It's off. Fausto said you don't stick to your agreements. He says you stitched him up that time at Turin." I said I didn't know what he was talking about but then when I thought about it everything made sense. I explained that I hadn't known anything about having 'sold' it, and had it out with Graglia. Once Fausto understood that Graglia had robbed us both we became firm friends again.

Bianchi and Legnano bossed cycling and sport is the same as politics – it's the bosses who make the rules. I didn't win as much but I was one of the first people to have the courage to fight against it. I could have had an easy life as a *gregario* for Coppi but that's not sport. You have to be able to look in the mirror and say you did your best and that you acted within the spirit of the competition.

Bartali? The worst thing in the world is a hypocrite and a liar who hides behind religion. Ultimately we're responsible for our actions not only to God but to ourselves and to those affected by them. Here was a person who claimed to have profound faith and yet spent his life lying and breaking promises.

The worst was a stage to Locarno, 1947 I think it was. I was riding with a broken collarbone and so I was out of the GC. Me, Coppi and Bartali were away, and it made sense that I had the win. Coppi agreed but then Bartali said: "Today is the anniversary of my brother's death. I think we should honour his memory, so it's best if I have the win." You can't really argue with that and so we gave him the win. Then we found out it wasn't the anniversary at all; it was two days later. That was disgusting to me, but it tells you everything you need to know about Gino Bartali...

——

Prior to Fiorenzo Magni's rise to prominence in 1948, Vito Ortelli was the 'third man' of Italian cycling. He won the Italian Road and Pursuit Championships and finished third at the famous Giro of 1946. As a professional cyclist he remained chaste for 43 months and 14 days.

"I had a lot of time for Coppi because he was serious, honest and professional. He took pride in what he did and he was totally concentrated on it..."

ENZO BELLINI

b Carmignano, 1924
pro 1946–1951

Ninth 1948 Milano-Sanremo
Eleventh 1948 Giro di Lombardia
Three Giri d'Italia, all finished

I finished the 1948 Giro, Magni's famous 'Giro of the Pushes'. I was on the Pordoi that day and so I can tell you exactly what happened. There were three stages to go and my team-mate, Ezio Cecchi, had the jersey by 2'18" from Magni. Coppi was at eight minutes and Bartali was out of contention altogether. I remember that it was a very cold day and there had been talk of re-routing the stage because of the snow. I was a pretty decent climber, so they told me to stay with Magni for as long as I could, to keep an eye on him.

Coppi needed a miracle, so he attacked on the Falzarego and was away up the road. I say he needed a miracle but if I'm honest nothing would have surprised us where he was concerned. Cecchi was a better climber than Magni and when I watched him ride away from him on the Pordoi I thought that it was done and dusted.

Cecchi was winning the Giro but all of a sudden people started pushing Magni – they were lined up along the roadside and every 100 metres or so they were shoving him! Magni was losing the Giro, no question, and it was shameful what was happening. It was orchestrated and that was the worst thing of all. As a bike rider the biggest indignity was to accept being pushed and if people tried to push me I would be livid. And yet here was Magni screaming at people to shove him up the thing. I was shouting at them to stop because I couldn't believe what I was seeing but they weren't paying any attention...

Cecchi still got over the top before Magni but then he punctured and crashed on the descent. Magni had two team-mates with him, Cottur and Bresci, and they worked like fury, obviously. Bartali was with Cecchi but for some reason he refused to help him. I don't know why but what I do know is that if he had Magni wouldn't have put those five minutes into him. The jury fined Magni two minutes, which left him in the *maglia rosa* by 11 seconds.

The rules stated he should have been expelled not because he'd been pushed but because he'd *allowed* them to push him. Some said the people pushing were employees of Wilier, his team, but I can't confirm that. What I do know is that Coppi would have been second on GC had they thrown Magni off but he was so disgusted that he left the Giro. I also know that we lost the Giro by 11 seconds.

My first season was 1947, with Welter. I was earning factory money really but I was a professional cyclist, contracted to a team. There were nine of us and the objective was to race as often as we could and to try to get in the seven who rode the Giro.

I'd say there were probably about 80 salaried professionals in Italy. Then you'd have another 120 or so independents, blokes trying to make a living from riding their bikes. There were maybe another 30 Italians spread across Europe, but mainly in France. Some of them were essentially itinerant cyclists but others rode for French teams.

I rode the Giro, and the team did well. Bresci won a stage and finished third on GC; Cecchi was fourth, Martini sixth. In effect, though, there were two races going on. Coppi and Bartali were racing one another for the *maglia rosa* and everybody else was trying to win a stage or do the best they could and earn some money. I finished 41st out of 50 or so but I finished. I never had any pretensions of becoming a champion...

Our problem was that we never had a sprinter. People like Leoni, who won four stages, did very well for their team-mates but we couldn't afford him. He would have been on double what I got and somebody like Bartali would have been earning at least four or five times as much, plus prizes and appearance money.

There was a strike at the Giro that year, the first ever in cycling. It was on the stage to Rome and they were making us ride on horrible dirt roads when as often as not there was a new asphalt one running parallel. I've never seen so many punctures in my life and I've never been so scared on a descent. It was ridiculous, as if they were trying to make us crash on purpose just to create news stories.

I had the best day of my career at Lombardy in '48. I went over Ghisallo with the best of them and then I beat Bobet in the sprint at the Vigorelli. It was the sprint for 11th but Bobet was still a champion, wasn't he? Coppi came over to congratulate me personally for the way I'd ridden and I was on cloud nine. Fausto had ridden it on his own, as usual. He won it four times in a row, didn't he? I think he won that day by about six minutes...

▬

Enzo Bellini never won a professional race, but within the Tuscan cycling community he is revered. Most everyone I spoke to told me he was one of the most decent, selfless human beings in cycling.

"Coppi came over to congratulate me personally for the way I'd ridden and I was on cloud nine. Fausto had ridden it on his own, as usual. He won it four times in a row, didn't he? I think he won that day by about six minutes..."

GIOVANNI CORRIERI

**b Messina, 1920
pro 1941–1957**

*Winner of seven Giro d'Italia stages
Pink jersey 1953 Giro d'Italia
Winner of three Tour de France stages*

Bartali and I roomed together at the Giro and the Tour and often we'd sleep in the same bed. He'd talk and talk and mainly he liked to talk about himself. Eventually I'd nod off – I got used to falling asleep with the lights on. He'd sleep for two or three hours because that was all he seemed to need.

On the final stage of the 1948 Tour I was in a break with Lucien Teisseire. On the last climb I was really clinging on because he was an exceptional rider. He offered me 50,000 francs for the win but I turned him down. Then he offered me 100,000 francs but I said no because I knew that if I won I would earn much, much more at the criteriums. I also knew that the Parc des Princes would be full of Italians.

I beat him easily and Bartali famously won the Tour. Afterwards we set off to ride all the criteriums together. We spent the month driving all over France and Belgium, 30 races in about 30 days. If memory serves Bartali was being paid a 500,000 lire appearance fee and I was getting about 50,000. That was still a lot of money, a month's wages for a day's work. He always drove and he hardly ever slept. He'd be driving all through the night and he'd be smoking. I'd nod off and when I woke up he'd still be prattling away. When he was tired he'd pull in and sleep for maybe ten minutes, then he'd be off again.

At the 1949 Giro, the famous Cuneo-Pinerolo stage, I was there when Coppi went. I shouted at Gino because I knew it was going to happen but it was too late. Coppi knew that Bartali's Achilles' heel was the first 100 kilometres. When he got warmed up he was amazing and I maintain that he was a better climber than Coppi. Coppi was better on the flat and better against the watch, mind.

Gino was always hung up about money. He'd sleep in cheap hotels, and he was convinced that people were trying to rip him off. I'd say: "Look, if you look after people they will look after you. It doesn't need much, but you have to have people on your side to win the Giro. Look at Bianchi!"

He wouldn't have it though. He'd say: "I don't buy races, and I don't sell them!" He was as stubborn as a mule sometimes, and it cost him.

Sicilian Giovanni Corrieri moved to Tuscany in 1940. For seven years he was Gino Bartali's most trusted *gregario* and confidant. He rode six Tours de France and famously outsprinted Bartali to win a stage at the 1951 Giro.

"Bartali and I roomed together at the Giro and the Tour and often we'd sleep in the same bed. He'd talk and talk and mainly he liked to talk about himself…"

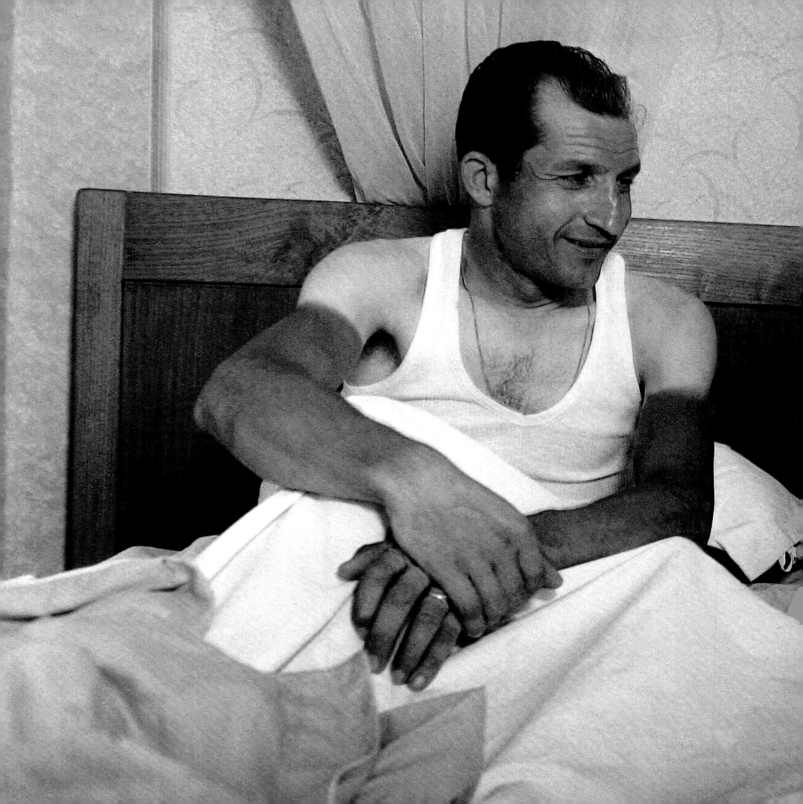

ALFREDO MARTINI

**b Sesto Fiorentino, 1921
pro 1941—1958**

*Pink jersey and stage winner 1950 Giro d'Italia
Stage winner 1951 Tour de Suisse
Winner 1947 Giro dell'Appennino*

The 1948 World Championship in Valkenburg was the height of the Coppi and Bartali rivalry. I'd also say that it was, without question, one of the blackest days in Italian cycling history.

From my point of view it was my first World Championships. I was 27, and riding for my country had always been my big dream. Selection for the *Azzurri* back then was hugely important because the competition was so fierce, much more than today. They chose eight to go to Holland and from those only six were to ride with the other two reserves.

Essentially what happened was that Bartali won the Tour and so they gave him leave to arrive late because he was running around France riding all the criteriums. That left the seven of us there preparing, each hoping we'd make the team.

Gino arrived and all seemed pretty normal. The issue was that he and Coppi weren't communicating with each other at all by now. We were all used to that but this time it was so strained between them that Coppi took himself off altogether. He figured that if he stayed away from the hotel there would be less tension.

Bartali had won the Giro in 1946, Coppi the following year, but when Bartali won the Tour and seven stages it topped everything. The point is that every time one or the other won the stakes got higher – great champions like them weren't in the habit of conceding ground. You'd also got the commercial interests of Legnano and Bianchi at play, because when one or the other won it had a direct impact on bike sales. Had Bartali won the rainbow jersey so soon after the Tour it would have done wonders for Legnano's sales and by extension it would have been disastrous for Bianchi. There was speculation that Coppi hadn't even wanted to come to Holland but that Bianchi obliged him to go to stop Bartali winning.

For some reason Alfredo Binda, who was the manager, wasn't there that year. They gave the job to Lugari, a guy from the federation, but he didn't have a clue how to handle the situation. He couldn't unite the team, though to be fair to him it would have been impossible anyway. In effect each of them was going to ride for himself come what may, and if that meant riding to stop the other winning then so be it.

So the fact was that neither of them was ever going to accept playing second fiddle. What's interesting about the race – and what people tend to forget – is Magni was there as well. He'd won the Giro, he was in the form of his life, and the *percorso* was 340 kilometres. The Cauberg was the main climb, and so it was perfect for his characteristics. Realistically, in the circumstances he was probably our best bet for the win.

You know the rest: Magni and I were the ones left out. To be honest it wasn't a huge problem for me, nor a surprise. The riders we had were all exceptional, people like Ortelli, Ricci and Luciano Maggini. I couldn't really complain about not riding but Magni was deeply upset. You could hardly blame him.

The race itself was a disaster. It suited both that the other didn't win and so they simply watched each other rather than going for the win and risking the other taking it. When the break had gone they just sat there and then they both abandoned. They were both suspended by the federation for unsportsmanlike conduct and we were a laughing stock. Both Magni and Bartali retired never having won the World Championships and Coppi had to wait until 1953 to take the rainbow jersey.

I didn't have a problem with either of them but I tended to get on well with everyone anyway. I was much closer to Magni. We were the same age, both Tuscan, and we'd ridden for Bianchi together during the war years. It might seem strange to you but I still believe that in many respects his was the best career of all. He won the Giro three times and yet by his own admission he wasn't in the same class as Coppi and Bartali. Nobody else was either but because of his intelligence and his fighting spirit he found a way to win three Giri in which Coppi participated.

Don't forget that Magni would have won the 1950 Tour as well. He had the *maillot jaune* and in my opinion he was stronger than Kübler. Bartali decided that the team should withdraw and so once again Fiorenzo was the big loser.

——

Alfredo Martini wore the *maglia rosa* for a single day in 1950. An excellent racer in his own right, he was principally famed for his skills as a diplomat. He helped Fiorenzo Magni (twice) and Gastone Nencini win the Giro, and was present when Coppi won the Tours de France of 1949 and 1952. Later he would become Italian national team manager. He and Magni remain "like brothers".

"**The point is that every time one or the other won the stakes got higher — great champions like them weren't in the habit of conceding ground...**"

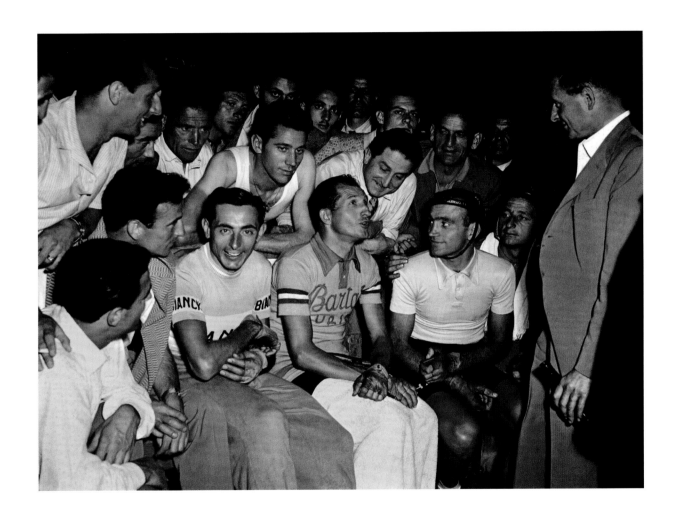

ARMANDO BARDUCCI

b Martorano, 1926
pro 1949–1956

Stage winner 1952 Tour de Romandie
Runner up Giro di Toscana, Trofeo Matteotti
Third in four Giro d'Italia stages

© Original author

I am happy to talk, though I don't really know why you want to speak to me. It's not like I was much good.

Something always seemed to go wrong. I'd have a mechanical, or a puncture, or somebody would break a promise. There was always something and whenever there was some money to be made I managed to find a way to miss out. I guess I was just born unlucky, a born loser.

It was hard. My dad was a land worker but he struggled to find work. He'd do a couple of days, then miss a couple. Three days on, three days off. I wouldn't say we went hungry, but we didn't have anything. I had one older brother and four younger sisters but all my siblings have gone now; I'm the last one.

I left school when I was 12 and started work as a plumber. The standard working week was six days but I did Sunday mornings as well because we needed the money to live. Up until I was 18 I'd get up at 5am, train on the bike for a couple of hours, then go to work for eight hours. In the evening I'd go to technical college between 6pm and 8pm.

The days were full and I was always running around, always busy. I used to look forward to Sunday afternoons because that was when I'd go to watch the bike race with my mates, or ride to the beach at Cesenatico. Obviously we'd be racing one another, as all kids did, but I couldn't afford a racing bike. I had a 'sporting' bike, but with racing handlebars. I was the strongest of our gang and I started wanting to race.

I think the first race I did was in 1946 and I've an idea I finished about sixth, something like that. Anyway I was lucky for once because Mario Vicini lived 200 metres from us. He'd been second at the 1937 Tour de France, third at the Giro, and he had a bike factory in Cesena. He said: "I'll make you a bike and you can pay me when you have the money." That was how I knew I had to get serious. I needed to earn some money to be able to pay for it!

So I decided to take out an amateur licence. I won a few but I lost a hell of a lot more. I was strong, I was full of desire, and I recovered really quickly. My problem was that I was worse than useless in a sprint, so I always got beaten. To be honest I could lose a sprint against my own shadow.

I started professionally in 1949 and I rode the Giro six times. I did five with Frejus and one with Legnano. I only ever won once as a professional, a stage at the Tour of Romandie. I also won the team prize at the Tour of Switzerland, with Ferdi Kübler and Jean Goldschmit. I liked Kübler because he was a good bloke, and Romandie and the Tour de Suisse were the best races. The house we're in now was basically a three room hut, but with the money I made there in 1950 we managed to make it into something. I'd have been on 50,000 lire a month then, and I reckon I would have earned about 800,000 that summer.

I remember a lot of the races because I found so many ways to not win. At the 1952 Milan-Sanremo I was in the break with Robic and Alfredo Martini. We got to the bottom of the Berta and I was the strongest, so I left them and I was on my own. The bunch caught me, as I knew they would, about a kilometre from the finish. I didn't mind so much because I was going to get a good result, or at least good by my standards. And then of course I cramped. 11th...

You signed your contract at the big bike fair in Milan. I remember getting off the train there once, on my way to sign for Legnano. As I got off the train I saw Minardi. I said: "Where are you going?" and he said he was off to sign with Magni's team. You earned a better salary there but Magni was getting on and so I figured he probably wouldn't win so much. At Legnano we had Defilippis and Albani and so I said: "No, come with me to Legnano. We'll do really well and you'll earn more money." I managed to convince him to come and of course Magni won a load of races that year. Minardi had the pink jersey at the Giro for a couple of days, but then he crashed and broke his collarbone. We never earned a bloody thing.

I don't know if Coppi, Bartali and the like had agents, but I know they had their own personal doctors. We *gregari* had doctors as well – they were [amphetamines] called Stenamina and Simpamina!

Of the champions I'd say that Bartali was the one I didn't get on so well with, because he'd say one thing and do another. Magni was all right, but Fausto was my friend. He wasn't one of those who thought he was some kind of a God, not at all. He was a champion but he was also just a good, honest man. When he came to ride here in Romagna we always went hunting together. He was good company, Fausto.

At the Giro di Toscana there were three of us in the break and I dropped the other two – I was really good that day. Anyway they caught me on the descent and then there was the final climb, the San Baronto. Magni jumped and so did about five others. Fausto came up to me and said: "Get on this if you can because it's the winning break. You'll regret it if you don't go with it." I got second behind Magni but I'm convinced I was the strongest in the race that day...

I suppose I was quite well known round here. I wouldn't say I was famous though, not like the footballers today. I remember a particular Giro d'Italia, when there would have been about six or seven of us *Romagnoli* riding. Round here they never called me Barducci but 'Bardoz', local dialect. Some of the others – Minardi, Ortelli, Ronconi – actually won races, and yet everybody seemed to be cheering for me. All the journalists were asking: "Who's this 'Bardoz' character? He's not on the start list" and so people were explaining that it was me, Barducci.

When I finished I went to work for Vicini and I was there for 28 years. When I retired my nephew took my place.

I still don't know why they cheered for me and not the others and I still don't know why I was always on the front. I've been thinking about it all my life and still to this day I don't understand it. Instinct I guess. Or a curse...

▬

One of the most generous *gregari* of his generation, Armando Barducci rode professionally between 1949 and 1956. He started the Giro d'Italia six times and never failed to finish. He lost his brother in a cycling accident. He lives in Martorano in the house he grew up in.

"He wasn't one of those who thought he was some kind of a God, not at all. He was a champion, but he was also just a good, honest man. When he came to ride here in Romagna we always went hunting together. He was good company, Fausto…"

RENZO ZANAZZI

b Gazzuolo, 1924
pro 1946–1952

Stage winner 1946 Tour de Suisse
Stage winner 1946 Giro d'Italia
Two stages and pink jersey 1947 Giro d'Italia

Pictured left © Original author

The 1950 Giro? I'll try to explain...

Learco Guerra was from Mantua, like me, but like me he lived in Milan. He lived just here, 200 metres away, and his bike factory was just up the road. So we knew each other well, and obviously he had his team. He said to me: "What type of rider is he, this Hugo Koblet?" I knew Hugo well, and I told Learco that he was a thoroughbred. He didn't really know how to ride but I told Learco that if he could manage him properly he had the physical capabilities to win the Giro. Physically Koblet was a sensational specimen.

The Giro was to finish in Rome and the winner was going to have an audience with the Pope. Coppi had crashed out and Bartali was obviously the poster boy of the church. Therefore it suited everybody that he win but Koblet was much better. The problem was that no foreigner had ever won the Giro, let alone a Protestant. Anyway it was the penultimate stage, Campobasso to Naples, and Koblet had the jersey.

There was a 'flying' stage at Isernia, a type of intermediate sprint. All the best sprinters went for it, and we had 300 metres on the group. I won it but immediately afterwards I punctured and so everybody came by me. I waited for the Arbos team car to come up and give me a new wheel but it never came. I assumed that somebody else had a mechanical back down the road and changed the tub myself.

As I got back on the bike I looked back and saw the pink jersey. I thought: "Jesus! How much time has he lost here? He's going to lose the Giro!" He was pulling as hard as he could and there were two or three sitting on. They weren't doing a turn though and he was giving it everything to try to get back to the Bartali group. He didn't say a word but he didn't need to. He and I started doing bit-and-bit, with the others just sat on. After a while I could tell he was really suffering and so I said: "Hugo! For Christ's sake eat something!" He said: "I've had five punctures, Renzo, and I missed the feed!"

I always had a packet of sugar lumps in my pocket and I gave him them, ten or 12 sugar lumps. At a certain point he started pulling again and so the sugar had obviously helped him to survive the crisis. We got back on eventually but it was touch and go for a while. Magni told me that Bartali's team had pulled like crazy and so Hugo had been in real danger of losing the Giro. We were right on the limits.

That night at the hotel I saw Hugo on the stairs, wearing his Learco Guerra tracksuit. He pulled out a roll of Swiss francs and I said: "Put your money away, Hugo. I didn't do it for that, and I don't want it." He said: "Look Renzo, if it hadn't been for you I'd have been finished. You deserve more for what you did but this is all I have. Take it, please..." He wouldn't take no for an answer and so I put the money in my pocket. I earned more in those 80 kilometres than in the two years I'd spent working for Bartali.

I'd had four motives. I wanted to get back on for me, obviously, but also to give Koblet a hand because he was a good guy. He was riding for Learco Guerra, and as I said before he and I were friends, and both *Mantovani*. The other thing was to get one over on Bartali, because he was such a despicable, loathsome individual.

The people who write all that stuff about him didn't know the real Bartali. I roomed with him a thousand times and I know exactly what he was like. They created this big hero but he wasn't like that at all. He was totally selfish and totally ignorant and he was forever breaking promises. To be honest he was also a lousy bike rider. He was a fabulous climber, no question, but he was a hopeless leader. As a *gregario* you were always having to waste energy fetching him because he always rode at the back of the group. I swear that if he'd had half the intelligence of someone like Magni he'd have been twice the rider he was.

The first stage of the 1947 Giro, Milan to Turin, I broke away on my own and won by 2'33", stage and jersey. By stage five Bartali had the jersey and we were headed to Florence, his home town. He said: "Renzo, don't tell the others but you'll need to lead me out in the sprint today. We're finishing at the Stadio Comunale and all my family will be there." Then Bini, another of my Legnano colleagues, said exactly the same thing. Finally Ricci, the sprinter, said I needed to lead *him* out as well! I was supposed to lead out three different sprinters! I made sure I got in the break that day, and I won the stage myself.

1952, Roccaraso to Ancona. I was riding for Ganna, for Magni. The stage started with a descent and Ambrosini, the race director, said: "Look Zanazzi, we want to neutralise the descent because it's dangerous and it looks like rain. We'll just roll down it together, and start racing in the valley." I said: "Yes, but the route is what it is. I could understand if it was snowing, but it's not. The descent's horrible, yes, but how many horrible roads have we descended? How many white roads full of holes and stones have you sent us down?" We were there to race, not to muck about.

So we set off, and I was near Ambrosini's car. We got rolling down this thing and it started to rain. I looked round, the group had shrunk, and all of a sudden Coppi came by me in his *ammiraglia*! Then Bartali as well! All the bloody leaders were in their team cars! I said to Ambrosini: "What the hell's going on here? What are they doing in the cars?" He said, "There's nothing stopping you getting a lift as well, Zanazzi. We've just decided we'll start a bit further down the road, that's all." I wasn't having that but next thing there's only about 30 or 40 of us left on the road. We're soaked through, while the others are having a nice little trip. I wasn't having that either, so I said to the others: "What are we, a bunch of cretins?"

So when we got down the hill we stopped under a tree and made a bonfire. I was a bit of a shop steward back in the day, so I said: "Let's see how the Giro goes on with 40 of its riders missing..." The drivers gave us some petrol, and the farmers started bringing us logs. We stayed there a while and of course the whole Giro had to stop. When we got going I got talking to Magni. I said: "I bet Coppi had Ambrosini neutralise it because he's feeling rough. As soon as we start again I'm off. I'll make them chase and then we'll see how he is." We knew that when Fausto got ill he got *really* ill, so it was worth a try...

So I talked to a few of the others and we attacked straight away. Bianchi had to chase, which exhausted them, and so Fausto was left with no team. He came up to me and said: "What are you doing this for? It's pointless!" That really annoyed me and so I said: "Look, I ride for Ganna, not for you! I'm here to put food on the table, and I'll ride as I see fit!" He said, "Just pack it in!" and I thought, "*Pack it in?* Who the hell is *he* to tell *me* to pack it in? I'll give him pack it in!"

I was absolutely incensed and so I attacked again. This time nobody could hold my wheel and so I found myself alone off the front. Eventually Massocco came across and they caught us on the outskirts of Ancona but I made Fausto work all right. He saw to it that I didn't ride any of the track meets after the Giro and so I lost a hell of a lot of money.

Anyway that part of Marche has a big shoemaking tradition and after the Giro a big bag of women's shoes arrived, 25 pairs of them! They were some kind of combativity prize and Guerra said: "What have you done with all those shoes?" I told him I'd given three pairs to my sister, but that I'd become *very* popular with the girls.

The best cyclist was Magni. He wasn't a *fuoriclasse* like Fausto but he knew how to read a race like nobody I ever met and my God he knew how to suffer. His attitude was that if he was hurting himself then he was also hurting the others and that's why he was such a great rider. He was as hard as nails but he was absolutely straight.

I was generally fine with Fausto but I was good friends with Serse. I remember riding an amateur race against him in 1940 and he turned up in Fausto's pink jersey! I'd say that of the two he was much, much the more intelligent; he was Fausto's brain.

There are all sorts of stories I could tell you about Fausto. There are things which Serse told me in confidence which I'll take to my grave. Some things are best left unsaid. Let's just say that Fausto was more or less as good as his word. Usually more, but sometimes less...

——

The oldest and most successful of three professional cycling brothers, Renzo Zanazzi rode for Gino Bartali's Legnano team in 1946 and 1947. Early in his career he won three Giro stages and was considered a champion in the making.

"I was good friends with Serse. I remember riding an amateur against him in 1940 and he turned up in Fausto's pink jersey! I'd say that of the two he was much, much the more intelligent; he was Fausto's brain..."

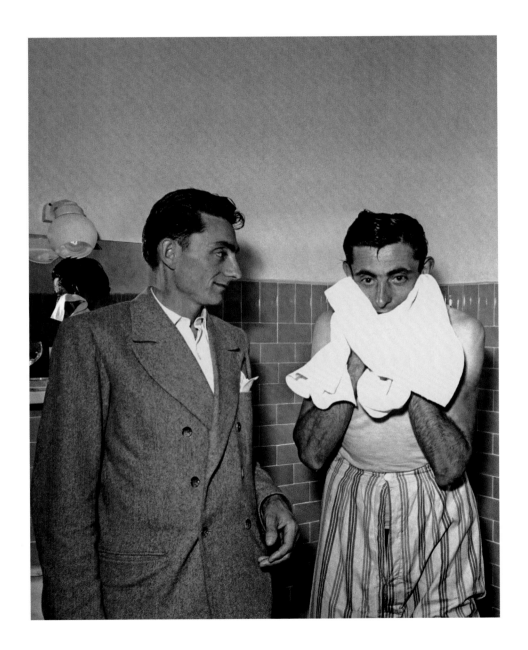

RENZO SOLDANI

b Cireglio, 1925
pro 1949–1955

Winner 1950 Giro di Lombardia
Winner 1950 Giro dell'Appennino
Winner 1950 Giro dell'Umbria
Winner of three stages of 1950 Giro di Puglia

I grew up at Cireglio, in the hills above Pistoia, and I idolised the cyclists. I remember seeing the Giro come by when I was a kid and for me people like Guerra and Binda were celebrities, like film stars.

Cycling was very popular round here and before the war the battle had been between Bartali and Aldo Bini. Bartali was from Florence and Bini was from Prato, just up the road. Before they turned pro they'd been racing each other pretty much every week and so the rivalry wasn't artificial at all. They were both brilliant riders and they genuinely didn't like each other. Everybody was captivated by it.

As regards my own career, I'd say I sparkled briefly, but no more than that. I was an excellent descender, one of the best. I had no problems on the flat, and I was reasonably quick. As regards climbing, if I trained and took it seriously then nobody could drop me. The truth though – and my great weakness – was that I was more interested in women than cycling. I couldn't help it; I just liked them a great deal, and they seemed to like me. If I went to Sardinia there would be a woman, if I went to Rome another...

The point is that I was born into poverty. When I say that what I mean is that there were days when there was nothing to eat, no bread. There's no shame in admitting it now; the fact is that we went hungry. They were millers on both sides of the family. Mum and Dad, aunties and uncles; the mill was your life. There were six of us kids and when my dad fell ill we had no way of getting money.

In 1943 I was 18, and I got a letter saying I needed to present myself for military service. I didn't want to go though and so I didn't. The Americans were still down at Cassino and the Germans were building the Gothic Line here to stop them advancing north. The group organising it was called Todt and there were thousands of us working on fortifications, digging tunnels and such like. I didn't like the Germans but it was better than being sent off to war.

Our house was isolated, high on a hill, and one day we had a visit at home from the Fascists. They said: "You have to evacuate this house because it's the sort the partisans use to hide out. We're going to have to demolish it, so the sooner you leave the better." So now my sister and I were effectively refugees but as chance would have it someone offered us a place to stay in the forest. My papers were a week or so out of date and the local women told us the Germans and Fascists often did round-ups in the area. If you didn't have the documents, or you'd avoided going to the front, they'd cart you off to a labour camp or whatever. The next morning I set off for town to renew my papers, so that I could prove I was working for Todt. And as I walked round a bend I found them in front of me. "Hands up!" That was that...

They put me on a work gang, then I was sent to Carpi for a medical. From there they transferred me to Verona, then on to Frankfurt on a freight wagon with about 20 others. There was another medical and they decided which front you were to be sent to. Some were sent to Russia but I was lucky because they sent me to Metz. I dug anti-tank craters but the Americans were three kilometres away and the front kept being pushed back. It was obvious they were winning and I managed to escape with about 15 others. We had to hide for 15 days, and one by one the Germans picked them off. Me and two others held out though and when the Americans did their next big push I was able to turn myself in on their side. They gave me a uniform and it was exactly the same as theirs except that it said 'ITALY' on the sleeve.

I had to pinch myself because it was as if I'd woken up on the set of a Hollywood movie. I'd never seen anything like it and I'd never lived so well in my life. There was all the bread you wanted, meat, margarine, potatoes and fruit. Then they had chocolate, chewing gum, cigarettes. I didn't have to do anything, just drive a truck, and at the end of the month they paid me! I'd never seen so much money. There was no way I could spend it all, so I just used to chuck it in a suitcase. Anyway eventually the war ended. I carried on working for the Americans for as long as I could but in 1946 it was all done and so I had to come home.

Just before I'd been sent away I'd ridden a bike race and I'd really enjoyed it. Then while I'd been in France I'd been to watch a few races and I'd decided that when I got home I'd get a bike and try again. The problem now was that I had no money, and a decent racing bike cost 13,000 lire. Luckily somebody told me that you could exchange foreign money and I remembered that I had a load of French francs kicking about somewhere at home. I took them to the bank and they gave me 16,000 lire! I went straight to Susini,

a local pro who also had a bike shop, and bought a bike.

So that's how my cycling career began, aged 21. I had no choice but to enter open races and so I was up against independents straight away, people who'd ridden the Giro. In the first race I stayed with the front group and I got joint sixth, and from then on I started winning.

By the end of the season I was doing well for myself. The races tended to start in the afternoon and so I'd ride there, do the race, then come home. I spent the whole summer on my bike because I rode everywhere. I'd set off at sunrise and get home whenever. I remember a race at Castelnuovo di Garfagnana, 100 really hilly kilometres away. Then the race itself was 160 kilometres, then home again in the evening. I dropped everybody and I remember thinking that it was easier to win the race than it had been to get there. I did 43 races that year and I earned enough to buy a horse for the mill.

I was winning a lot and it got me an entry for the Tour of Piedmont at the beginning of November. That year it was reserved for second category professionals, independents and amateurs. I won it and I beat people like Carrea, Coppi's *gregario*. Legnano offered me a contract and so I became a professional bike rider. Later on people would say to me that I'd gone to university without having gone to high school and they were right. I'd done seven years' worth of riding in two.

I won some smaller races that first year and I was always in the top ten or so. I did well enough at the Giro and then I won the Coppa Placci, which was an important one. The journalists started writing that I was talented. Apparently I was going to replace Bartali at the top and so Legnano tripled my salary to 900,000 lire. That was a colossal amount for somebody like me.

In August and September 1950 I won a lot of races and so by the time Lombardy came round I was floating. The favourites were the same as ever – Coppi, Bartali and Magni, Koblet and Kübler. Then you had the outsiders, and I was in that group with Fornara, Ortelli and Bevilacqua. When Coppi attacked on Ghisallo I was the only one able to stay with him and so there we were, him and me. Our *direttore sportivo* Pavesi had told us the night before that if we got in a break with any of the stars we should avoid pulling. I didn't like the idea of that but I soon realised that Coppi was a class apart. If I'm honest he was doing 500 metre turns and I'd maybe do 100. It looked like he was happy to tow me to the Vigorelli, and he was so good that I was on the limits just to stay on. I was in the form of my life but he was something else entirely. He was phenomenal...

As we got into Milan, Pavesi came up and told me to start pulling because Zampini and Bevilacqua were getting across to us. Bevilacqua was a very good sprinter but by the time they reached us he'd given everything. He had nothing left and so I came round him and Fausto and won the sprint easily.

It was the last race of the season and it was the first time since the war that the Coppi/Bartali dominance had been challenged. Koblet and Kübler had won the Giro and the Tour, Magni had won a lot, and I'd won ten races including Lombardy. They had the Desgrange-Colombo Challenge back then, effectively a world cup. Kübler won it, from Magni and Koblet. Coppi and Bartali were fourth and fifth but they were 31 and 36 years old respectively. Conclusion: I was the future of Italian cycling.

Legnano had offered me a 1.8m lire salary before Lombardy but we hadn't agreed anything. Now there was a new team, Taurea, and they were offering 2.3 million. Legnano had no choice but to match it and so I stayed put. The win bonus was 300,000, with 500,000 for Sanremo or Lombardy. To put that into perspective, a nice apartment cost about 800,000.

Bartali was nicknamed 'The Grand Duke of Tuscany' round here, and before the war Bini had been 'The Duke of Montemurlo'. Now they started calling me 'The Count of Cireglio'. I went out and paid one million lire in cash for a car and bought myself a new wardrobe from the best tailor in Pistoia. The following year I bought an Aurelia B20 Sport, for 2.2m lire. If you'd put Coppi and Magni's cars together they'd have been worth about that. As a kid I'd seen cars but the idea that I might one day own one had never occurred to me. Now I had one, and it was the best one there was. It was just beautiful.

Cycling was very big in Argentina and they wanted the best riders to go over and ride a series of track meets, no expense spared. They selected the best seven Italians and I was one of them. I travelled first class with Coppi, Bartali and the others, and we had the best of everything. The best hotel in Buenos Aires, the best women, a dinner party with Eva Perón...

I was being paid a fortune but I didn't believe I was in the same class as Coppi, because I'd ridden with him. That was the point about that Tour of Lombardy. I won but I knew I was out of my depth with Coppi. In retrospect it was also the beginning of the end. It earned me more money than I could have imagined and it tricked people into thinking I was something I wasn't. Riding with Fausto that day taught me that he was a class above and that even if I trained like him I could never be that good. The other thing, as I said, is that I wasn't actually that bothered: for me it had started to become a means to an end.

A priest once said to me: "You know, Renzo, that you didn't ever realise your potential. You had all that class and yet you didn't become the cyclist you could have been." I said: "You're absolutely right. When you joined the church you gave up everything else. You married the church, but I was busy chasing women. I never married the bike, and nor the life of a cyclist. I was far too busy having a good time for that..."

Following his defeat of Coppi at the Tour of Lombardy, Renzo Soldani outsprinted Gino Bartali to win Sassari-Cagliari, the opening race of the 1951 season. The media frenzy that followed saw him installed as favourite for Sanremo, but at Milan-Turin Coppi brought him down in the sprint. He finished well down at Sanremo, and would win only once that season. Now a new star, Loretto Petrucci, emerged as the local favourite, and Renzo failed to win another professional race. The Count of Cireglio retired in 1955.

"**I travelled first class with Coppi, Bartali and the others, and we had the best of everything. The best hotel in Buenos Aires, the best women, a dinner party with Eva Perón...**"

FRANCO FRANCHI

b Teramo, 1923
pro 1949–1955

Stage winner 1950 Giro d'Italia
Runner up 1955 Giro di Sicilia
27th 1952 Tour de France

Leading the peloton © Publifoto/Olycom

I was there when Serse crashed in Turin, right behind him. I could see what was going to happen and I shouted "Look out!", but it was too late. He rode back to the hotel though and so obviously we thought nothing of it. Then we found out that he had died...

The first Tour de France I rode was 1951, a few days after. I remember being at the hotel in Metz, on the eve of the *départ*. Bruna was pleading with Fausto not to ride and it was one of the saddest things I ever saw. She was begging him for hours. His morale was destroyed but in the end he sent her away. He was a professional cyclist and he had to ride.

At the 1952 Tour Coppi was doing things I could never have imagined. I think it was probably the greatest exhibition I ever saw. My most vivid memory is a stage down in the Pyrenees, somewhere near Lourdes. The road had been resurfaced and the problem was that it was so hot that the tarmac was melting. The bike felt like it was sinking.

Anyway it was one of those stages where you knew you were going to have a terrible time, because you'd spend all day fighting. Essentially your job was to get water for the leaders first and then you thought about your own thirst. The captains couldn't stop at a fountain and get water, obviously, because everybody would have attacked and they'd have lost. That's why we were called watercarriers and that was the job – to get water.

So everybody was suffering from this terrible thirst, just trying to get through as best they could. There was a fountain and so I stopped to fill everybody's *borraccie*. Van Steenbergen attacked just as I stopped, and so the race went away from me. That meant that I had to chase to get back on because if you didn't you risked being *hors delay*. I buried myself for 20 kilometres, desperately trying to reach the back of the group, holding onto cars, you name it. It was insanely hard, but I made it back on.

Before I could drink I had to get the water to the captains. Obviously the water was warm, because it had taken so long for me to get back on. Coppi and Bartali were riding together if memory serves and I apologised to them for the water being warm. It was no big deal, because they knew I was doing my best. Then I went to Magni and gave him the water. He said "It's warm!" and then

I watched him throw it away. I couldn't believe what he was doing! I'd suffered like a dog to get that water and he threw it away because it wasn't fresh! That water was so precious and so I said: "Well that, my friend, is the last time I will be fetching water for you." I'd had enough of being treated like a slave. I was going home.

Magni and I both rode for Ganna, and Luigi Ganna called that night. He said: "Stay there. I'll come tomorrow and we'll straighten it out." He spoke to Fausto about what had happened and after that I was treated really well. I was given a new jersey and shorts every day while Magni wasn't, by way of punishment.

—

Franco Franchi completed the 1952 Tour de France as a *gregario* for the winner, Fausto Coppi. One of very few successful racing cyclists from the southern Italian region of Abruzzo, he has fond memories of his amateur racing days but not of the way he was treated as a professional watercarrier.

"At the 1952 Tour Coppi was doing things I could never have imagined. I think it was probably the greatest exhibition I ever saw…"

135

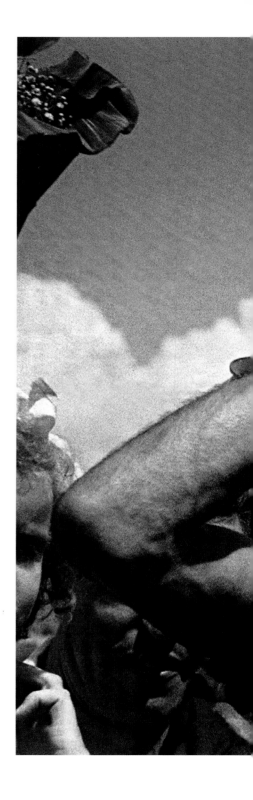

GIUSEPPE MINARDI

b Solarolo, 1928
pro 1950–1958

Winner 1952 Giro di Lombardia
Stage winner Giri d'Italia 1951-1956
Pink jersey 1954 Giro d'Italia
Runner up 1952 and 1955 Italian national championship
Runner up 1952 and 1953 Milano-Sanremo

© Publifoto/Olycom

O
ur good fortune was that we lived in the country, not in the town. Therefore we weren't bombed and we didn't have to evacuate. We grew our own wheat, milled our own flour, made our own bread. I always made sure that I saw the sun rise rather than vice versa.

I wasn't interested in sport and I certainly wasn't a cycling fan. I started bricklaying and so I needed a bike simply to get to work. I didn't start until I was 18 and I think I was lucky in that respect. You can't have 13-, 14-year-old kids riding vast distances because it's no good for their bodies at that age. Cycling's terrible when you think about it because your instinct is stronger than you and you go beyond the limits of what your body can handle.

So that's how I got started and I found I was quite good at it. The other lot had all these beautiful racing bikes with drop handlebars, the best tyres and so on, but I just seemed to ride mine quicker. They were saying: "Pippo, how can you ride that thing like that?"

Anyway I started racing and I found I could win. At that point I had to decide whether I wanted to be a cyclist or a worker because the guy from the cycling club said he would give me a wage to ride. I wasn't happy about it though, not at all. The idea that I would get paid a wage for riding a bike was absurd and so I said: "I'll take it, but only because I need some kit and if I'm doing cycling I won't have an income to buy it. And I'm only accepting it on the basis that it's a loan. If I'm good and I win then I'll pay you back out of the winnings. If I don't win then I'll get a job, and I'll pay you back out of the wages." He was a bit shocked but he accepted. I won a lot, because I was lucky. What I mean is that it didn't seem to matter what speed the others did because I found I could always go faster.

1951? The stinging nettles? How did you know about that? I suppose it's quite a funny story, but you need to understand the context first. The first thing to bear in mind is that there were no transfers back then. Because they wanted the Giro to reach as many of the regions as possible, sometimes we'd have to ride these ridiculous, monumental stages. That day we did Foggia to Pescara but we didn't take the coast road. Instead we did 311 kilometres, up and down all day with three really big climbs. The other thing to be mindful of is that it was hot down there and that it was stage ten, the last before the rest day.

As usual the journalists had been saying that it had been a boring Giro. They'd been predicting that the stage was so long and hard that it was bound to blow it up, but of course days like that always had the opposite effect. Obviously there was no way you could go hard over that kind of distance during a stage race because nobody would have got round. What tended to happen was a tacit agreement to take the day off and to just enjoy being on our bikes until maybe the last 50 kilometres or so. We'd ride at 30kmh, and nobody would attack. That was nice for us but it made it dull for everyone else. For the people listening on the radio and the journalists it was terrible, still more so for the caravan and the race organisers.

Anyway we were riding along nice and easy and it must have suited everybody because after 270 kilometres there were still about 60 of us in the front group. I was riding at the back and Pavesi, our DS, came up. He said: "Come on, Pipazza! Do something! It's boring!" and the next thing I knew he was hitting me on the back of my legs with a bunch of stinging nettles, laughing his head off! So obviously I started moving up into the belly of the group, just to get out of the way of that lunatic with his stinging nettles...

I carried on to the front to have a look at what was happening and then I got in the break with Padovan, Barducci, Franchi and Bizzi. I won the sprint and so that was my first Giro stage. After that I won one every year until 1956, six editions in a row. They said it was some kind of a record, but I also managed to abandon five on the bounce, between 1953 and 1957...

It's a nice story but it wasn't that I won the stage *because* of the stinging nettles. It was just one of any number of little things that happened on a day where, ultimately, nothing at all happened. Essentially you had a load of journalists following the race and each of them was looking for some kind of a story. They weren't going to get it from the racing itself, nor from the GC blokes. Therefore it had to come from the stage winner and that's why they jumped on Pavesi's little comedy sketch.

That's the way it always was with cycling. All the journalists had to get copy in and so they'd blow things out of all proportion or just invent them. There was no TV, so it wasn't like you could watch an action replay. I'd reckon half of what was written about my career was made up...

My abiding memory? Bizarrely enough it's probably my first Giro, the one when I *didn't* win a stage. I remember it because I won 15,000 lire, and because I accumulated 20,000 in fines. Welcome to professional cycling, Minardi...

▬

As the sun set on the careers of Vito Ortelli and Aldo Ronconi, Faenza produced a third great rider, the hugely popular Giuseppe 'Pipazza' Minardi. He won extensively, but following his retirement from the professional sport never again rode a bike.

"That's the way it always was with cycling. All the journalists had to get copy in and so they'd blow things out of all proportion or just invent them. There was no TV, so it wasn't like you could watch an action replay…"

148

RICCARDO FILIPPI

b Ivrea, 1931
pro 1953—1960

World amateur champion 1953
Winner Trofeo Baracchi 1953, 1954, 1955 (with Fausto Coppi)
13th 1954 Milan-Sanremo

© Original author

I n 1950 I signed for SIOF. I went to live in Novi Ligure and we lived the life of professional cyclists. We had the same jersey as Bianchi and they gave us bikes, board and lodging. It was essentially a finishing school and the idea was that the best riders would progress to ride for Bianchi. I was there for three years and from my group Favero, Gismondi and I were the three who made it. The rest weren't up to it, so they signed elsewhere or didn't turn professional.

As amateurs we weren't salaried and the money we won went straight back to Biagio Cavanna. Obviously out of that they paid for our keep. Cavanna may have been blind but he knew cycling. He lived and breathed it, and he thought about it all the time. While we were out training he would be coming up with new ideas. I always thought that a person who can see has a lot of other stimuli, but he couldn't and so he didn't. He was pretty relaxed but if you tried to play him he'd find out, and he could be pretty hard. If you said you'd trained for 150 kilometres and you hadn't he'd get to know. Don't ask me how, but he did. You couldn't cross him because if you did you were crossing Fausto.

I won the Amateur World Championship at Lugano, 29 August, 1953 and Fausto won the pro race the following day. I beat Gastone Nencini in the sprint and he went on to win the Giro and the Tour. If you ask me why Gastone became a star and I didn't it's a little complicated, but I'll try to explain as best I can...

After I'd won the championship Fausto and I won the Trofeo Baracchi two-up time trial together, both of us wearing our rainbow jerseys. It was the last race of the season and it was a very, very big event. Suddenly I was riding with my idol, we were both world champions, and we were becoming really close friends. It was as if I'd been chosen.

The first race the following spring was Paris-Nice, and I was second in two of the stages. As far as I was aware I was doing a good job, but for some reason they decided to clip my wings.

At Milan-Sanremo I was flying, and I got in the break with Stan Ockers and Raoul Rémy. I was much stronger than either of them and every time the road went up I was having to wait. I said to them: "Look, give me a hand when you can, but I'll pull on the climbs. That way we'll get to the finish and we'll all be on the podium." The proviso was that I'd win the sprint but we all agreed that's what we'd do.

Then Tragella, the DS, came up. He said: "Stop pulling, because Fausto has attacked on the Berta. He's got 100 metres and he's trying to get across..."

So now I had to sit up, even though I was going to win, and of course they caught Fausto so it was all a waste of time. They caught us about three kilometres from the finish and so now you had all the sprinters, people like Petrucci and Van Steenbergen. Petrucci had won the previous two editions for Bianchi but he'd had to leave because Fausto couldn't accept anybody else winning. He was going for his third Sanremo and that's why Fausto had Pino Favero grab hold of his saddle. Fausto was there as well but he was never much of a sprinter. His rationale was that he didn't mind losing to Van Steenbergen but there's no way Petrucci was going to win again and become an even bigger star. There was no way I was going to win either because if I did it would damage his power base. That was how it was; everything was calculated to ensure the status quo was maintained, and who was I to go against Fausto Coppi?

You know the story of the Stelvio? At the 1953 Giro? Okay, so you know that Nino Defilippis helped Fausto to win the Giro that day. Two years later there was a stage to Sanremo, and Nino attacked. He was riding for Torpado and I was with Fausto, with Bianchi. There was always a little bit of rivalry between me and Nino because he was from Turin and I was from Ivrea, just up the road. I asked Fausto if it was all right for me to go across and he told me that I had to stay put. Nino won the stage unopposed...

Don't get me wrong. All the riders respected Fausto and as long as everybody knew their place he was fair. Basically on flat stages he'd close the race down and then at 20, 30 kilometres from the finish he'd let people go. That's why most riders were on good terms with him. He gave them the crumbs and they were content with that. That's the way it was – Fausto dominated the cycling world.

They tended not to take me to the Giro and I wasn't one that recovered really well over three weeks anyway. I wasn't a stage racer but believe me when I tell you that I could have won just about any other race...

Within the team we all got on pretty well. The only one I would say I had issues with was Carrea. He guarded his position close to Fausto and he was jealous if anybody else was close to him. He was an exceptional climber but he wasn't up to much on the flat. Milano was a much nicer guy, almost like Fausto's butler. If his shoes needed cleaning he'd be there cleaning them.

We won the Baracchi three times together, Fausto and I, three in succession. Then in 1956 we were second, beaten by Graf and Darrigade. The reason, if I'm honest, was that Fausto wasn't as strong as he'd been previously. But as far as the media were concerned when we won it was because of him and when we lost it was because of me.

The following year I automatically assumed we'd be riding it together again but he never said anything. We were training together, as always, but it wasn't confirmed and then I got the flu. He rode it with Baldini and won but I was left with the sensation that the organisers wanted them to ride together regardless. Baldini was the new star and Fausto hadn't won for two years, so obviously it was good business for everybody.

I suppose the fact is that after a while you lost enthusiasm to even try to build a career of your own. If you ask ten times and the answer is always no, the 11th time you don't even ask the question, do you? You're essentially just a servant, but at the same time you're being paid. That's why I never really thought about leaving. There was an implied threat that if you did the same thing might happen that happened to Petrucci, or De Santi, and so you just carried on.

Fausto always said I should have done more with my career but of course that was a contradiction in terms because it suited him perfectly. I'd set off full of enthusiasm that first spring, and now you know what happened.

When I retired I got a job at Olivetti straight away. I was thankful for that because there was no pension as a cyclist and I needed to work. As a bike rider you had a contract but you were basically freelance – if you didn't ride you didn't get paid.

I have no regrets. I didn't become some great champion but I had a good life after cycling, a good marriage and two healthy kids. I had a decent career and I've nothing to reproach myself for.

▬

Fausto Coppi missed Filippi's wedding in November 1959, sending a note saying he had an engagement he "couldn't avoid." Devastated by the news, Riccardo said this was one of the most painful moments of his life.

"You're essentially just a servant, but at the same time you're being paid. That's why I never really thought about leaving..."

PINO FAVERO

b Settimo Torinese, 1931
pro 1953–1959

Winner 1953 Milano-Busseto
Runner up in four stages of the Giro d'Italia
Third 1954 Milano-Sanremo

© Original author

When I was 16 or 17 I was already riding with the amateurs, though technically I wasn't old enough. I should have been doing junior races but they let me be. I was working in the family bakery but they offered me 30,000 lire a month, which was a working wage. I trained with a local professional, an independent named Savioli. He taught me to ride, sorted out my position, what to eat, all that stuff. We rode together every day.

I was riding for the Fiat Railways Division team in Turin. They took us to the races in an open-backed truck, a Fiat Balilla with benches in the back. I would go really well in training, much better than the others, but every time I raced I threw up. I couldn't understand it but they just said: "Look, there's something wrong with you. Maybe it would be better if you got yourself sorted out and then tried again later."

They stopped paying me but it transpired there was nothing wrong with me – it was the exhaust on the truck! I got sick because I spent the entire journey inhaling exhaust fumes!

So I went back to training alone, or at the velodrome, and I signed up to ride Turin-Chiavari. It was an open event, amateurs and professionals together. I was only 18 but I dropped them all and won.

Three weeks later there was a letter for me, from Biagio Cavanna. It said I needed to present myself at Novi Ligure for a meeting with SIOF, Bianchi's feeder team. So I went along and he started touching me. He started feeling my arms, and I had really strong arms because I was a baker. He shouted to his wife: "Irma! I've found us the perfect gardener!" They decided they wanted me and I decided to give it a go in the knowledge that if it didn't work out I'd always have a job in the bakery. I moved in there in January 1951 and that was where I would live for the next six years. I roomed with Riccardo Filippi, and that was my life. I'd come home for a month in the winter but aside from that we lived together and rode together.

We were a really strong team and I always won because I was fast and nobody could drop me on the hills. I think I won 31 races in a row, something like that. People started asking me where I'd be riding on the Sunday, so they could find a different race to do.

We'd ride all the most important races in Italy and we'd win them. We didn't get paid but if you were good enough you were guaranteed a place at Bianchi. There were four or five of us who were permanent there, but at any given time there would probably be half a dozen others. They would pay to come for a trial in the hope that they'd be good enough to stay. Most didn't last a month.

At SIOF all the others rode Bianchi bikes but I rode a Girardengo. I used to play cards with him twice a week and he gave me a bike. That aside we lived exactly as Coppi and the others did; all of us eating, training and living together. The only difference was that at the weekends we'd separate for the races. The professionals would go their way and we'd go ours.

In general the training was constant. One day you'd do 240 kilometres, next day 130, 220, whatever. We were supposed to be turning our legs over to stay in shape for the races but sometimes it got a bit much. I remember once I cleared off during training because I was bored of them attacking each other for no reason. I hid behind a house and waited for them to come by. They spent all day looking for me and I arrived an hour late. Fausto wasn't happy about that. He said: "You can't do that Pino, it's taking the piss." I said: "No, but it's ridiculous everybody attacking each other all the time. Sometimes we need to do recovery rides."

We were living with Cavanna but it was Fausto who decided things. He was timid and he wasn't the type to argue but he was ultra-professional and very precise. He was obsessed about the bottles being clean and he would check them every morning. They were tin and you didn't throw them away like they do today. Everybody was responsible for his own but by the same token he might need to drink from mine, me from somebody else's and so on. It was the same with food. You had to eat the right things, in just the right quantity, at exactly the right time.

Someone like Bartali would smoke, drink grappa, stay up half the night, but we were highly disciplined. Bear in mind that the stages were much longer. These days they'll start at midday, but we used to roll out at 8am. You'd need to be eating your pasta at 5am, so you'd be in bed early in the evenings. Maybe you'd be listening to the radio but you'd be resting. In theory you were free to come and go as you pleased but we were professional athletes and Fausto led by example.

We were a really compact group and everybody had his role. At the Giro, for example, I had to watch people like Bevilacqua and De Santi, the ones who always tried to go away on the flat. Generally Carrea pulled on the climbs, and Milano had to stay close to Fausto to protect him in the group. Then me, Filippi and Gaggero would fetch his water, give him our wheel, whatever. Often I'd stop to get the water, then chase like hell to get back on. I'd give it to him and he'd laugh. He'd say "But it's warm, Pino!" and I'd say: "Yes, but it bloody well wasn't when I got it!" He'd say: "Listen, do me a favour and stop at the next bar. Get me a nice cold beer." He'd drink a couple of mouthfuls and give me the rest...

That story about me pulling Loretto Petrucci's jersey in the sprint at Sanremo is rubbish. It's true that I was marking him all day, and it's true that Coppi had an issue with him. He'd basically said to Bianchi: "Either Coppi goes or I go" and so obviously Fausto would be angry about that. He was the greatest cyclist on the planet, while Petrucci was just a very good sprinter who had won Sanremo twice. Anyway I never touched him, and nor would I do that to any other rider. I just led out the sprint, that was all, and I finished third.

For me Fausto was right. When Petrucci left Bianchi he never won again and while he was with us he didn't pull his weight. When there was work to be done he was never there.

Fausto and Bartali got on very well, but bear in mind that by the time I came along Bartali was practically finished. I can't say I really knew him but I heard that he was tight. Aldo Bini, for example, rode for Bianchi and for Bartali, and he hated Bartali – he said he owed him a fortune.

The point about riding for Bianchi was that your salary was three times what you'd get elsewhere. Sure if you moved on you might be free to try to win and become a big star but what if you didn't? We were well off. I bought three or four apartments. Fausto's wage was exactly the same as mine, as everybody else's, and all the prize money was divided equally. His appearance fees, his sponsorships, all that was nothing to do with us, but our *direttore sportivo* Tragella told me that we all got the same, and he was no different.

Women used to throw themselves at Fausto, and he had a lot of them. Sometimes when we were out training after he'd won the Giro or the Tour, they'd be on their knees in the road. We'd have to stop, literally, so that they could touch him.

I'd often have to wait while he went off somewhere. He had a story with Katyna Ranieri, the famous singer, and he would often talk about that. In fact the only one he didn't talk about was the *Dama Bianca*.

Once when we were in France we rode to a hotel and he said: "Wait here, Pino. Keep an eye on my bike for a quarter of an hour." He went upstairs with this amazing, beautiful Brazilian girl. When he came down he said it hadn't been all that. She'd had bad breath, apparently.

In the autumn of 1954 I went to do a track meet with him, Magni and Piazza. We were on the train and that was when he told me the *Dama* was pregnant. He was absolutely furious, believe me. He wasn't interested in becoming a father again and he certainly never thought he'd be spending the rest of his life with her. She trapped him.

Bruna had always been like a mother to me and I thought the world of her. Every time I went round there she would say: "Have you eaten something? Do you want me to cook you something?" She looked after me but she didn't know how to be a *signora*. She was just a women who liked to be at home, to cook, clean and iron. He, being Coppi, wanted a woman who was always in order, a different kind of woman.

So Carrea and I were for Bruna, not for the *Dama*. My relationship with Fausto didn't change – we'd been together for so many years – but I remember once when Carrea and I went to the villa to pick him up for training she started insulting us, accusing us of having exploited him. That was the last time we went there. From then on we'd meet elsewhere, and he wouldn't talk about it any more...

There were always 150 people outside his gate. When I went there in the evenings I used to have to sign his photographs for him. We had been sat around one day, him signing some pictures. I said: "It's easy, your autograph", and that was it; he saw that I could forge it really well, and it became part of my job. I must have autographed thousands of those photographs...

When I look back I can't understand how we did it; how our bodies withstood it. I was doing 250 kilometre races when I was 15, then riding up Stelvio on 46×22. We did 300 kilometre stages on those heavy steel bikes, on those crap roads, and yet none of it bothered me at all. I never even gave it a second thought...

Giuseppe 'Pino' Favero rode for SIOF, Bianchi's feeder team, and later as a *gregario* for Coppi. He lived in Novi Ligure until 1957 but when Coppi formed his Carpano-Coppi team he, Riccardo Filippi and Sandrino Carrea went their separate ways. Pino stayed with Bianchi and moved back to Turin, his home town.

"Women used to throw themselves at Fausto, and he had a lot of them. Sometimes when we were out training after he'd won the Giro or the Tour, they'd be on their knees in the road. We'd have to stop, literally, so that they could touch him…"

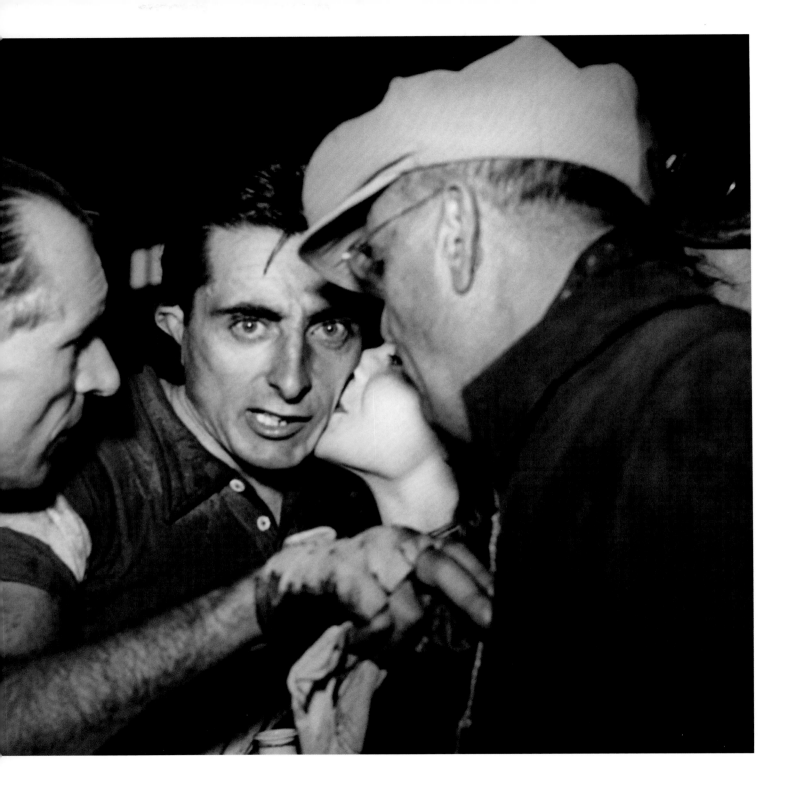

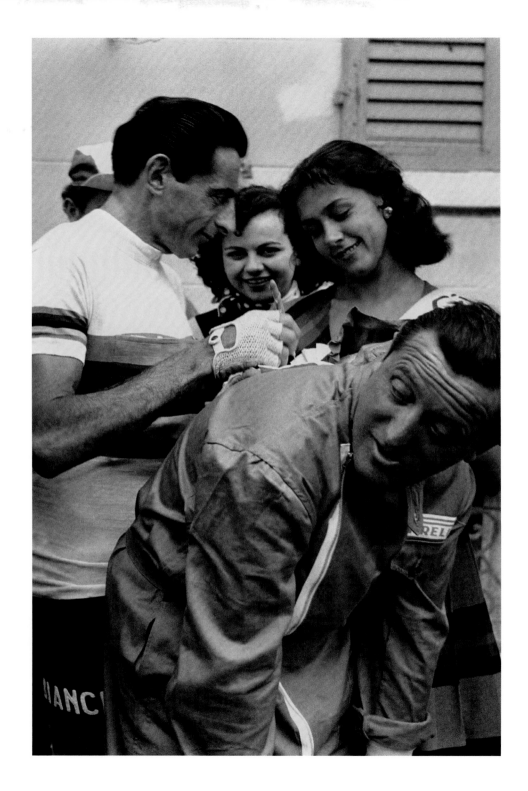

"**Bruna had always been like a mother to me, and I thought the world of her. She looked after me, but she didn't know how to be a *signora*. She was just a woman who liked to be at home, to cook, clean and iron. He, being Coppi, wanted a woman who was always in order, a different kind of woman…**"

NINO ASSIRELLI

b Forli, 1925
pro 1952–1962

Stage winner 1953 Giro d'Italia
Third 1954 Giro d'Italia
Stage winner 1960 Vuelta

© Olympya/Oly.com

I left school aged ten. We were country people, farmers, and so schooling wasn't considered to be of any real use to us. We kept pigs, maybe five or so, then sheep and some cows. You rented a bit of land and looked after the animals. That was what you did.

There wasn't a lot to do, so you rode. I started late, at 17, and I'd maybe win four or five races a year. I wasn't fast but I was strong, small and light. I recovered well and I could climb. I needed big climbs because otherwise they'd catch me on the descents. My specialty was long, long breakaways, because that was the only way I could win. I couldn't help myself when we hit the climbs. I just went.

When I was 25 I was offered the chance to turn professional with Arbos. The first season went well and I got them a lot of publicity because I was aggressive, even though I didn't win much. The team would have been seven or eight riders and so you weren't deciding who would ride what. You rode whatever there was because there were a lot fewer races.

I suppose that if I was famous it was because of those two long breaks. I guess you could say they saved my career in the sense that they created a lot of publicity and earned me reasonable contracts for the following year.

At the 1953 Giro we hadn't won any stages, nothing at all, and it had been a fortnight. We were in in the hotel in Turin and Giumanini, our DS, said: "Look, I've had the boss of Arbos on the phone and he says we're a disgrace. He says that if we don't make a decent fist of it tomorrow I am to retire the team and we have to go home."

Anyway there was a guy called Guido De Santi, and he was a kind of anti-Coppi. He was always attacking straight from the gun and that annoyed the hell out of Bianchi because he didn't play the game. De Santi was a very good rider but Coppi would never want him at the Tour, for example, because he would make everybody ride all day. I was near the front, and all the Bianchi lot were there watching him as usual. I was waiting and waiting, and then...

I went after seven kilometres; just gave it everything and prayed. There was a 100,000 lire combativity prize and to be honest I was only really trying to get that. We needed the publicity, and a bit of prize money for the lads. When I looked round I could see Piazza trying to get across. He was two metres tall and I thought he'd be a good bloke to be in a break with but he got to within 50 metres and then sat up.

It was so hot that day, and we had the rest day to follow. It obviously suited them to let me go for a while and I had no choice but to just keep going for as long as I could. And so that's what I did; I just kept going. For 225 kilometres. It was flat until Milan, which was hard, and then up and down to San Pellegrino Terme. I think I won by just under two minutes in the end.

Obviously they cut me some slack that day because if they'd decided to, they could have brought me back. I didn't create problems for the champions though and I made sure I didn't annoy them. I guess you could say that on that day it paid dividends, the fact that I wasn't a troublemaker.

The following year there was the famous breakaway with Carlo Clerici, when we took half an hour. He won the stage and the jersey, and ultimately the Giro itself. We'd agreed that I would get the stage though, and that he'd have the jersey. Anyway I hung on and finished third overall, and I think people appreciated the way I rode. I wouldn't say I was a hero, but of course the *Dama Bianca* story was breaking, and there was the riders' strike at Bernina. On the whole the Giro was a disaster for Italy and people said my performance was the one bright spot.

It was open season on Coppi because the Giro was such a massive event for the Italian public. It was his duty to win and as far as they were concerned he'd ruined everything by letting me and Clerici go. The only ones they weren't having a go at were me, Clerici and Hugo Koblet. We were portrayed as good examples, the others as feckless layabouts. I don't know if it was the beginning of the end for Coppi but I wouldn't have wanted to be in his shoes that last week.

My main memory of Coppi is that he didn't say a lot, but he was fine. He always said hello, and he was always polite.

—

Nino Assirelli's successful 225 kilometre lone breakaway at the 1953 Giro remains one of the longest in post-war history. The following year his escape with Swiss rider Carlo Clerici decided and defined the Giro. Its timing, allied to ongoing speculation over Coppi's extra-marital affair, was instrumental in a shift in the public perception of Fausto. Nino's brother, Alberto, won a mountain stage at the 1962 Giro.

"It was open season on Coppi, because the Giro was such a massive event for the Italian public and the *Dama Bianca* story was breaking... I don't know if it was the beginning of the end for Coppi, but I wouldn't have wanted to be in his shoes that last week..."

GUIDO MESSINA

b Monreale, 1931
pro 1954–1962

Olympic gold medallist 1952 team pursuit
World professional pursuit champion 1954, 1955, 1956
Stage winner and pink jersey 1955 Giro d'Italia

© Original author

I come from Monreale, near Palermo, and as a kid I worked at a bike rental place. I'd often have to go to fetch bikes that hadn't been returned, and I loved riding them. Anyway by the time I was 15 I was racing with the adults. Because there was barely any racing in Sicily everybody was just thrown in together. I found that I could keep up with them for half the race or so, even though they were grown men and I was just a boy.

I'm talking about Sicily in 1946, immediately after the war. It was very, very hard simply to survive. If you wanted to become a cyclist – or anything else for that matter – you really had no choice but to leave. Anyway a guy my dad knew was living in Turin, and that was where a lot of the cycling industry was. The guy said: "Look, send him up here and try, and we'll see how he gets on."

We were millers in our family and nobody knew anything much about sport. My dad thought it was a ridiculous thing to do. He couldn't understand that I'd want to come up here but my older brother managed to persuade him. My dad was relatively relaxed given that somebody from Monreale was looking after me, and to be honest I think he assumed I'd be home within a month. I think they let me come just so as I'd get it out of my system.

I was 16 when I came but bear in mind that I'd left school aged 12. When I got here I started working in a bike shop and I started winning straight away. I probably won the first 15 races I rode and I just seemed to be able to ride away from people. I'd never seen a velodrome in my life but the technical director saw me and decided I might make a decent pursuiter. I said I'd give it a go, and I did a really fast time.

They wanted to send me to the World Amateur Championships in Amsterdam but the problem was that I was only 17. I was too young to go but I forged the date of birth on my passport and went anyway. There was another Italian, a Bolognese guy called Benfenati. He was the reigning champion and he'd have been about 25. He wasn't at all happy that I'd been chosen, still less when I won the thing. He finished fourth.

I wouldn't say I chose the track as such – it just happened that way. All the decent sized cities had tracks and you earned well because people paid to get in. The velodromes were full and because people like Koblet and Coppi were riding pursuits it was a really popular discipline.

I was the world champion but I wanted to win an Olympic gold medal before I turned professional. I did that in 1952, and so by the time I turned pro in 1954 I was quite famous. My trade team was Frejus. They gave me a salary and a bike and I was expected to ride the road until the end of May, the Giro included. I was world professional champion three times in succession from 1954, and so my publicity value was high.

The two big track stars were me and Antonio Maspes, the sprinter who won seven World Championships. We were billed as 'The Two Ms', and when we were riding they were pretty much guaranteed a full house.

The first professional World Championship I rode was in Cologne. I won my semi-final, but there were only 45 minutes between it and the final, against Koblet. He was a massive star, right up there with Coppi and more famous still there because he was a German speaker. Nobody gave me a chance to win and to be honest I didn't expect to either. The semi had been brutal and I was destroyed physically. The place was in delirium for Hugo, and my main objective was not to get caught...

He was pretty arrogant, dismissive even. He set off like a train and within 1,500 metres I couldn't see him. It was obvious he was catching me, and at half distance he had 100 metres. I'd only just turned professional and as an amateur I'd always ridden 4,000 metres; I wasn't really attuned to riding 5,000. I knew how to ride a pursuit though and I knew that I couldn't afford to go into oxygen debt. By the bell we were equal and I beat him on the last lap. Had he not tried to catch me he would probably have won. I guess he paid for his arrogance. Three days later we did a track meet in Paris and he said: "I haven't slept since. I underestimated you, and it cost me the rainbow jersey."

We rode a lot. We'd ride the Sixes in Paris, New York, Buenos Aires. We had an agent in each country, and we'd pay them about eight per cent of our appearance fee. Back then a lot of the Tour de France stages would finish in the velodromes. Faggin, Maspes and I would go to Paris, Bordeaux, wherever, and we'd entertain the crowds. We'd start at 3pm and they'd pay to get in.

I won the Worlds again in 1955. That was when Strumolo, the organiser at the Vigorelli, started making noises about a pursuit with Coppi; a 'Match of the Century'. I was 24 at the time, and Fausto was 35. He was still Italian road champion though and he was still *the* cyclist. So we met, and Coppi said he wanted two million lire. That would have bought you two flats at the time but Fausto knew his value and he knew that the velodrome would be sold out. So Strumolo offered me 500,000 and I said that that would be fine but that I'd also be wanting 12 per cent of the gate money. He said, "No Messina, it's too much!" and so I said: "Okay, no match." I knew, and he knew, that it would be one of the biggest meetings of all time, and that they'd be making a lot of money. Anyway he agreed and we went ahead. Sunday 9 October, 4pm...

Vigorelli had a capacity of about 20,000 and by midday it was full, with another 5,000 locked out. They had to let them in and they sat on the grass in the middle. Obviously the point was that it was a pursuit so they had to remain seated so that Fausto and I could see each other. I beat him by 45 metres.

The following year I beat Anquetil to win my third World Championship and in 1957 I beat the great Ercole Baldini. For all that, when I reflect about what I did, beating Fausto was more important. I say that because it was a kind of unofficial World Championship, and also because of everything associated with the race. Most of all though I say it because he was him. He was Fausto Coppi...

The *Dama Bianca* was ambitious and she was very much into appearances. She was different to Bruna in that respect but Bruna wasn't just an ignorant farmer's wife by any means. She was a country person, yes, but she was a teacher and she was intelligent. By the same token Fausto left Marina, his daughter, and you don't leave your daughter if you're happy, do you? And you certainly didn't in Italy in 1954...

———

One of the greatest pursuiters of all time, Guido Messina won Olympic gold as part of the Italian team pursuit quartet, and five individual world titles. Among those he defeated were Fausto Coppi, Hugo Koblet, Jacques Anquetil and Ercole Baldini.

"So we met, and Coppi said he wanted two million lire. That would have bought you two flats at the time but Fausto knew his value and he knew that the velodrome would be sold out…"

PIETRO NASCIMBENE

**b Montalto Pavese, 1930
pro 1953–1961**

Stage winner 1956 Giro d'Italia
Stage winner and white jersey 1958 Paris-Nice
Stage winner 1955 Tour du Maroc

© Olympya/Olycom

I wouldn't say I chose to become a cyclist as such. I lived in a village and so like everybody else I used a bike to get about. Me and my twin brother were the youngest of six kids and my dad was a bricklayer. Obviously we weren't wealthy and so the bike was the only means of transport available. People rode them to get to work, to the shops, whatever. My instinct was to be competitive and so I suppose you could say that cycling probably chose me. I wanted to go as fast as I could, and truth of the matter is that I was strong...

Cycling was popular and bikes were popular and the sport was simply an extension of that. Of course you knew about football but as regards popularity it was nothing compared to cycling, believe me. Virtually every village, even the small ones, had someone who was racing a bike.

I wanted to be a racer but it wasn't at all easy for my parents to come to terms with. The perception was that cycling wasn't a proper career and that there were only three people making real money – Coppi, Bartali and Magni. Beneath them you had Defilippis, Astrua, maybe Fornara and the like, and then pretty much all the rest.

I wouldn't say it was something to be ashamed of but it was one of those pie in the sky ideas. You have to understand that on the face of it the chances of becoming a professional were pretty negligible. You'd be doing provincial races with 350 starters and there would be dozens of those races every Sunday all over northern Italy.

I didn't start racing until 1948. I was already 18 and so I had a lot of catching up to do. My dad saved up and got me a bike but because we didn't have a clue it was totally the wrong size. It was much too big and I didn't know how to ride but it didn't seem to matter. I started winning straight away.

My best memory in cycling is the 1953 Trofeo UPIM, an amateur race. There were 360 starters and I got away with a group of about 50 or so. There was an intermediate sprint at Cantù, and I won it. I looked round and I had about ten metres so I thought I'd try, like an idiot. There were about 35 kilometres to go to Milan and somehow I held them off. They were always at 20 seconds, half a minute, but I did it. It was the hardest time trial I ever rode.

I got the call from Legnano to turn professional shortly afterwards.

I'd won a lot that year, all the important races I entered, and so I was just hoping and praying that it would happen. I knew that if it didn't happen then it never would. When they said they wanted me it was like touching the sky with my finger.

So there I was, aged 23, and I was in Milan signing a contract with Legnano. My first race was Lombardy and so I'm riding up Ghisallo with Coppi, Magni and such like, my heroes...

The first race of the following season was Milan-Turin, 14 March. I came off and dislocated my thumb; wrecked it so completely that it barely works today. Back then you had no medical assistance whatsoever and five days later I had to ride Sanremo. I got round but I couldn't grip the bars and the pain was unbearable. Then I got a terrible saddle sore as well. It was a living hell but having spent all those years dreaming of being a cyclist I couldn't very well refuse to ride. It got worse and worse and to be honest I spent the whole season in agony. I won a couple of stages at the Tour of Belgium in August but Legnano didn't renew my contract.

I started 1955 riding as an independent. I was getting expenses and a jersey but no salary. You were basically riding for your future and so you went wherever you could and rode whatever you could in the hope you'd get another chance. The organisers paid your hotels and sometimes you'd be riding as part of an Italian national team, so the federation would pay your travel. At the Tour of Morocco, for example, there were four of us riding for Italy. We had no mechanical assistance, none of that, so effectively we were a bunch of mercenaries. That was it; Morocco, Catalonia – you rode whatever you could get. It worked for me because Arbos took me on and selected me for the Giro.

I got second at Trieste and third at Cortina d'Ampezzo but I never earned any money. People always assumed you did but you only did well if your leader was winning. If they did you divided the money but, if not, all you were dividing was the suffering.

I wasn't a big star and I didn't have a queue of people lining up waving criterium contracts under my nose when the Giro finished. In fact I went straight off to ride the Tour of Asturias. I won a stage there though.

At the end of the season I got a contract to ride for Fausto at Carpano-Coppi. It was a one-year contract but that was standard back then. In truth you weren't even paid for the full year, just the nine months you raced. I'd say that I was earning more than a factory worker, but not that much more. I reckon two months' wages for me would probably be equal to three months for him, plus whatever I scraped together in bonuses.

It was 1956 when I joined and you have to understand that 1956 wasn't 1949. The likes of Carrea and Milano, his *gregari* in the golden days, had done very well for themselves. Sure they worked and they were good riders, but the reality is that *he* earned *them* a lot of money. For me it was an immense honour to work for him, but he wasn't winning any more. The most I ever earned was at the 1958 Tour with the national team, not with Fausto.

You have to understand that he was *Fausto Coppi*! He was a God for us, and of course I was 11 years younger than him. I had always been a fan and still remember his first Giro like it was yesterday. It was 1940, and I'd have been ten. Obviously I grew up an hour away from Castellania and so naturally I'd supported him as a kid, as everyone round here had.

I never thought he fully understood who he was or what he meant, and I still don't. I remember once when we were trying to drive away and as usual when you were with Fausto there was a huge crowd. He was driving and I was in the back of his car. We couldn't move for people clamouring to touch him. He always kept a box of signed photographs on the back seat and he said: "Pietro, just wind the window down a bit and throw a load of photographs out." That was the only way to clear a path through them.

In Italian we have two ways to say 'you', two different ways of address. The formal *lei* is used as a mark of respect. You use it for people who you don't know, or people from a different social class. For people you know, people similar, we use *tu*. I couldn't bring myself to use *tu* with Fausto though, because it would have felt wrong. He used to laugh at me. He'd say: "Pietro, you can't address me with *lei*", but can you imagine being on intimate terms with God? That was what it was like.

——

Pietro Nascimbene won a stage at the Giro d'Italia, and still has his leader's jersey from Paris-Nice. He rode a single year as a *gregario* for Coppi and completed the 1958 Tour de France.

"I never thought he fully understood who he was or what he meant, and I still don't..."

222

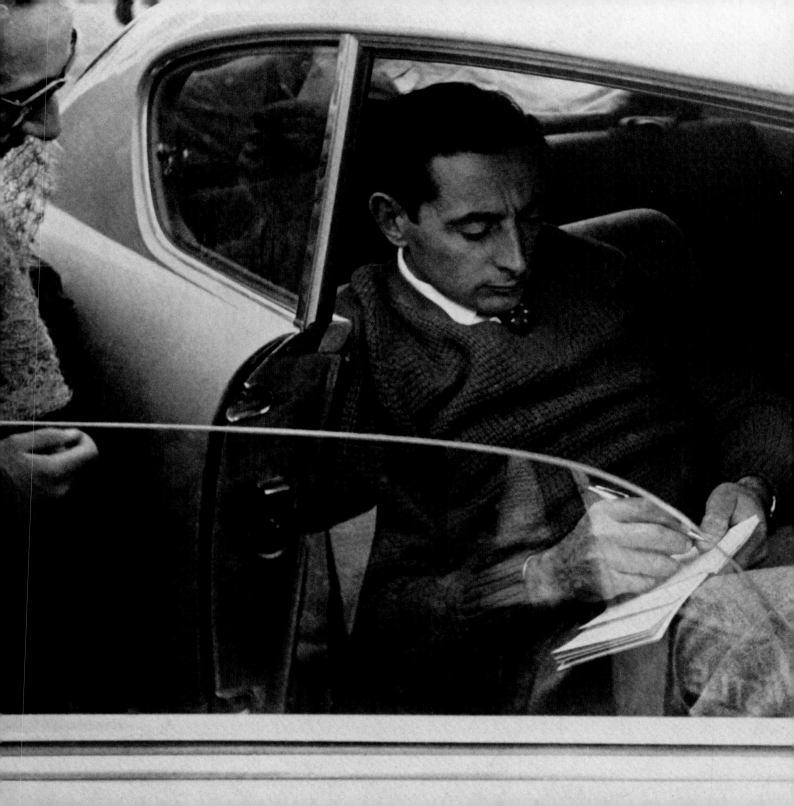

PIPPO FALLARINI

**b Vaprio d'Agogna, 1934
pro 1956—1964**

*Winner of two stages of 1956 Tour of the Mediterranean
Winner 1955 Mediterranean Games Road Race
Winner 1959 Gran Premio Industria e Commercio di Prato
Winner 1960 Giro del Lazio*

Pictured right © Original author

I was always pushing big gears, and it drove Fausto crazy. We'd do a 90 degree bend and I'd come out of it in 51×14, or whatever it was. He'd say: "Christ, Pippo, what are you doing? It's all right now because you're young but sooner or later you won't be able to do that any more. Remember that it's just like being in a car and the way you're driving you'll ruin your engine!" I'd say: "But Fausto, I haven't got a car. I don't know what you're talking about." Then he'd say: "Christ! This boy is crazy." He always said it just like that – "*Crrristoooo!*"

At Rome-Naples-Rome you'd ride the first part of the stage normally, then for the last 50 kilometres or so you'd be motor-paced. You'd mount a 58×14, something like that. I remember doing a descent at 120kmh one time. One day near Naples, Defilippis and I had twin brothers as pacers and they were insane. We were about equal on the road but these two maniacs were racing each other; carving each other up all over the road. We were exiting a curve and they actually brought each other down! Obviously it cost Nino and I any chance whatsoever but all we could do was to try to calm them down. They were out of their minds.

At the 1956 Giro I was second or third on GC for two weeks, never more than 90 seconds behind. I was virtual race leader no end of times and I nearly crucified myself to get that bloody jersey. I was almost there once. I could see the jersey before my eyes and then the chain came off 50 metres from the finish. Can you believe that?

A few days later I was in the break, virtual *maglia rosa* again, giving it everything. Now Magni came up, the great Fiorenzo Magni, and started making a scene. I'm not riding for his team, and so I say: "*Signor* Magni, why have you brought us back? It's my first Giro and you know I'm no threat to you."

So he says: "You can't keep trying to blow the race up – you're second on GC and you're just making life hard for everybody. I'm old enough to be your father!" I said: "To be honest you look old enough to be my *grandfather* but it doesn't mean you can tell me I can't pull!" Every time I moved after that he'd be on my wheel, laughing. He'd say, "Look, Pippo, your grandfather's sat on your wheel again!"

Fausto didn't say much but he was a good man. If somebody did him a favour, or if he liked someone, he made sure they were looked after. If that person tried to get in a break, for example,

Fausto would have Bianchi work for them or he'd organise it that the break stayed away.

I did the Tour twice, and twice I had to abandon. The first time I was virtual yellow jersey and I broke my collarbone, the second I got food poisoning in the Pyrenees.

It all started to fall apart in in the early '60s. At the 1961 Giro there were 170 riders, 15 Italian teams. Then they started to go bust, because the bike business was going bust. People were buying Vespas and Lambrettas and watching football on TV or going to the stadium. Bikes were old-fashioned, Coppi had gone, and all of a sudden there were only about six teams left. At the end of 1963, Molteni offered me 100,000 lire for ten months, where previously I'd been on 300,000. I wasn't going to ride for that. I had a family to feed and I couldn't afford to. People were walking away from the sport and so they didn't have enough riders for the Giro. Sixty or so new riders turned professional but they were earning lousy money.

Fifteen days before the 1965 Giro I was getting phone calls asking me to come out of retirement and ride, but I couldn't because I wasn't in shape. There were only 100 riders at that Giro.

——

Giuseppe 'Pippo' Fallarini rode professionally for eight seasons. He won two stages at the 1956 Tour of Europe, a ten day stage race between Zagreb and Namur. Two years later he won a stage at the GP Ciclomotoristico. A seven stage motor-paced race, it travelled 1,700 kilometres from Rome to Naples and back again.

"**Fausto didn't say much, but he was a good man. If somebody did him a favour, or if he liked someone, he made sure they were looked after...**"

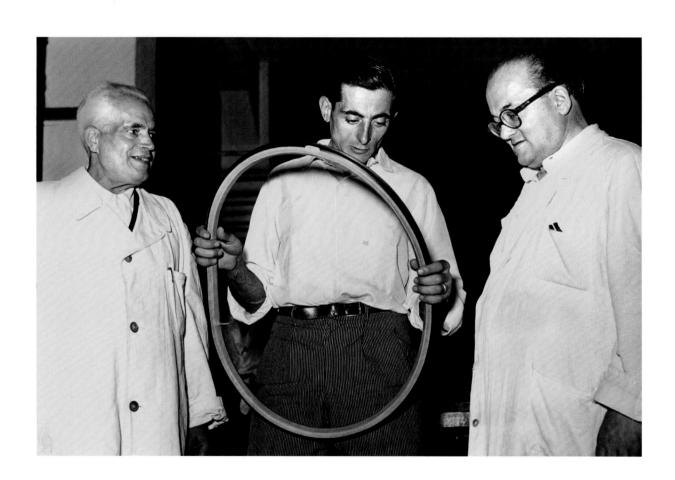

ERCOLE BALDINI

**b Villanova di Forlì, 1933
pro 1957–1964**

Winner 1958 Giro d'Italia
World road race champion 1958
Gold medal 1956 Olympic road race
Italian road champion 1957, 1958
World hour record (46.393kph) 1956

Pictured right © Foto Agenzia Omega Fotocronache Milano di Vito Liverani

Coppi was in decline when I started winning and so everybody was looking for the new star. There was Nino Defilippis, but he wasn't a stage racer, and so when I came along they started to write that I was the new Coppi. It started in 1956 when I won the Olympics and broke the hour record and carried on until 1958 when I won the Giro and the Worlds...

It was nice at the beginning. I was young and I felt really important but after a while it became a nightmare. To be honest I got to the point where I would just say "Yes, that's right, I'm the new Fausto Coppi," because I couldn't be doing with it; with the same boring comparisons. It's true that I was much stronger than the others and I was winning pretty much as I wanted. In the end I was so sick of talking about it that I just ended up agreeing with them.

The point is that they were in the business of selling newspapers. That's what cycling was about, and I was a means to that end. Even people who didn't know much about sport - or about Baldini - knew about Coppi and so the idea that there was a new one sold papers. Then, when this new Coppi 'let everyone down', they started to put the boot in.

In the main I got on pretty well with cycling journalists, people who understood the sport and reported on it. The problem was generally those who didn't understand it, those who invented stuff about my private life. They'd write that I'd been with other women, for example, and that obviously hurt my wife tremendously.

The truth, then, about my World Championship...

It was 1958, Binda was team manager and Coppi was his emissary on the road. Fausto couldn't win any more, obviously, but essentially Binda made it clear that we were to do whatever Coppi told us. More than just team captain, or leader, he was the manager on the road.

The basic premise was that if a small group went away we needed at least one Italian in it. If the group was bigger we needed two, but Fausto would decide who. So Bobet goes with Voorting, the Dutchman, and Gastone Nencini goes across immediately, as per Fausto's instruction. Nencini had already won the Giro and he was in excellent form, while Bobet was getting towards the end of his career and Voorting wasn't in their class. So although it was very early it seemed the ideal situation for us. We'd just be able to sit tight, block stuff and try to protect the break. Then at a certain point Coppi came up to me and said: "You go as well. Go and join the break..."

He was telling me to go but it made no sense for us. I said: "Why do I have to go? There are only three of them and Gastone has it covered." He said: "Yes I can see that, but you need to go as well. Go on..." I said it wasn't fair and that Nencini would be angry if I went across but Fausto wasn't having it. I had to go across...

So I caught them after two kilometres or so and Nencini asked me what I was doing. I explained that I hadn't wanted to come across but that Coppi had insisted. Nencini shrugged his shoulders and didn't say anything. Maybe he thought Coppi was a cretin, but he wasn't the sort to say anything. Anyway at that point the break was born.

I pulled more than the other three put together. Voorting didn't do anything, and if Bobet and Nencini pulled at 44kmh, I'd pull at 46. I didn't think for one minute it would be successful because there were still 260 kilometres to the finish but on the other hand I had plenty of energy and it wasn't like you could get any nasty tactical surprises there. I convinced myself that even if they caught us after 100 kilometres, people would at least realise we'd made the race. The Italian public tended to be quite critical of the *Azzurri* when we lost, particularly if we lost without trying to win. I wanted to at least demonstrate that I'd done my best, and so I went to work.

Voorting was the first out and so now we were three, me doing most of the work. We stayed away but by the time we were 50 kilometres from the finish the other two were barely contributing anything at all. Nencini said: "Look Ercole, I'm empty, but if I were you I'd attack Bobet now. He looks stuffed, but he's just put something in his bottle and so it may be that he'll be hard to drop in 10 kilometres or so." I thanked Gastone, he wished me luck, and then when we got to the climb I jumped.

I dropped them both but while Nencini climbed off, Bobet carried on. I'd been pulling for 200 kilometres but I rode the fastest lap of the entire race, on my own. I put two minutes into Bobet but then the gap didn't change at all for the final two laps. I beat him by just those two minutes and so maybe Gastone was right; maybe whatever it was he put in the bottle did give him a lift.

Here's something I didn't tell anybody for 30 years, and this is the key. Afterwards the story of the race wasn't that I'd won, or how I'd won, but about how Fausto had read the race so perfectly, how he'd been so intuitive. Apparently I'd been able to deliver the World Championship for Italy because of Fausto's intelligence and astuteness. Sending me up the road 260 kilometres from the finish had apparently been a masterstroke.

What was interesting was that Defilippis, who was my big rival, was the only one honest enough to come out and say it. Nino said: "That's right, credit Fausto because he chose the right moment, when in fact he was hoping that Ercole would blow up. Nobody in their right mind would go 260 kilometres from the finish and Fausto actually admitted as much within the group, in broad daylight." Fausto effectively admitted that he'd sent me on a suicide mission.

He was still just about the biggest draw for track meetings and such like but he was losing his grip. His thinking was that if I won I'd become even more famous and that would have a direct impact on his earnings and status. The more money I took the less there was for him and so it was just a business decision.

It happened though and it was the same between me and Nino. We were really big rivals and that's what made us the cyclists we were. When Van Looy won in 1961, Nino might have beaten him had I led him out, but why would I? I was in decline, and had Nino won it would have been detrimental to my career. I was looking after my own interests as the biggest rider in Italy, just as Fausto had been.

Notwithstanding the fact that we were rivals, my personal relationship with Fausto was generally pretty good. We'd won the 1957 Baracchi together and there hadn't been any particular issues. I didn't get on at all well with the *Dama Bianca*, however, and so she probably had something to do with what happened at the World Championship. She probably said: "Look it doesn't matter who you make win, as long as it's not Baldini." I was a threat, and I know for a fact that she resented me.

I don't mind the fact that Fausto sent me, because it was logical for him. What bothers me is the fact that still, all these years on, journalists continue to misinterpret what happened and why. Coppi sent me because he wanted me to lose, not to win, and he even admitted as much.

To conclude this thing you have to consider the net result, and also to be honest. Of course I was the strongest that day and in truth there was nobody to touch me. Regardless of Fausto's motives, however, the fact remains that had it not been for him I might not have won. A break could have gone while I had a puncture, I could have made a tactical error, whatever...

For a number of reasons I stopped winning as much in 1959. I still finished sixth at the Tour, and I still won some races. I wasn't a waster any more than I'd been the new Coppi but I couldn't stop the press slaughtering me and I certainly couldn't change public opinion. I'd been this new God of cycling and apparently now I was nobody, or even less than nobody. That's not easy to deal with, particularly for a young man of 26. They were hard years, believe me.

I'd say that there was only one occasion in my career that I struggled to hold a wheel on the flat. It wasn't Coppi, and nor was it Anquetil or Rivière. It was Romeo Venturelli on the first stage of the 1961 Giro. He was the new Fausto Coppi as well, for a few weeks. Then it was Zilioli, then Motta, then Gimondi...

——

In 1956 Ercole Baldini won an Olympic gold medal and smashed the hour record. The following year, now professional, he became Italian champion and won a sensational Baracchi Trophy in tandem with Fausto Coppi. It was Coppi's last professional win, and it came two years on from his previous victory, the 1955 Giro dell'Appennino. In 1958 Baldini won the Giro and the World Championship Road Race.

"Fausto couldn't win any more, obviously, but essentially Binda made it clear that we were to do whatever he told us. More than just team captain, or leader, he was the manager on the road..."

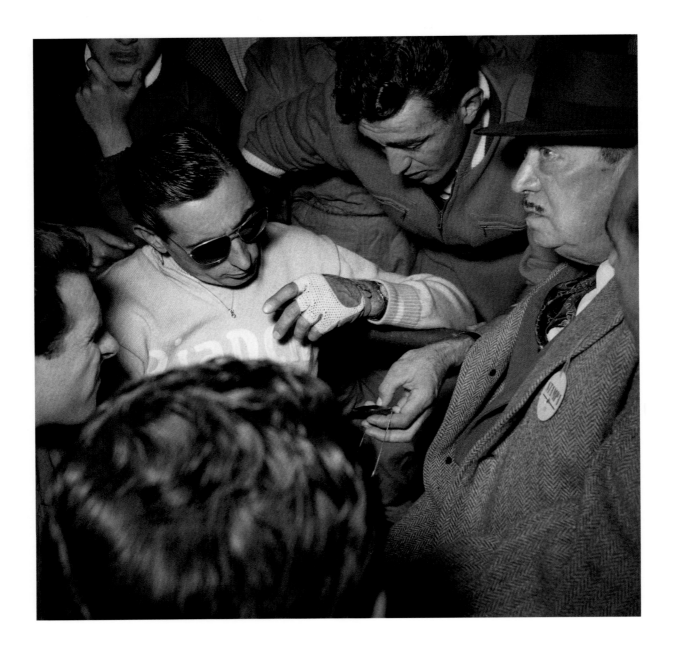

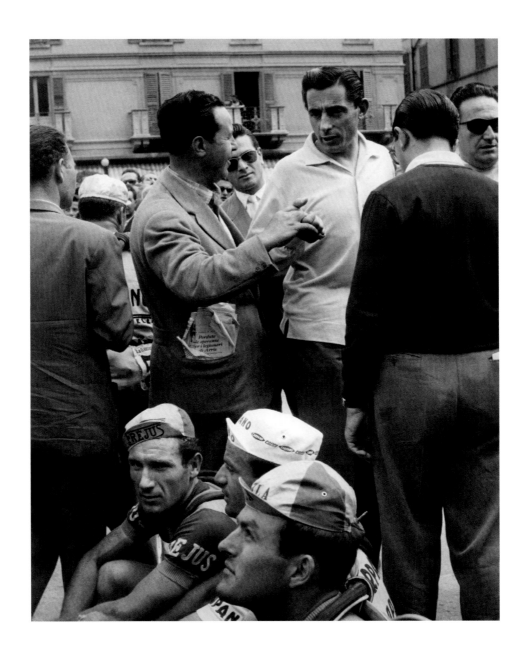

262

PAOLO GUAZZINI

**b Narnali di Prato, 1935
pro 1958—1962**

*Italian independents champion 1958
Winner 1958 Gran Premio di Pontremoli
Winner 1958 Gran Premio Mastromarco
68th 1958 Giro d'Italia*

© Publifoto/Olycom

My dad had a bike shop, and so I grew up in that world. I joined the juniors in 1951, aged 16. The problem was that we didn't have a car and so the *direttore sportivo* wasn't much good to us really. Anyway that's not the point. The point is that I was fast but I was a nail on the climbs. I kept getting dropped and it's obviously quite difficult to win when you're out the back. They said: "Look Paolo, we're going to send you to Novi Ligure to see Biagio Cavanna. He'll sort you out."

Cavanna was already blind but he was Coppi's masseur and apparently an expert on young cyclists. He had his team, SIOF, and people said he was some kind of Svengali. I did as they said and caught the train to Novi. He asked me some questions and I said: "I love cycling but I'm hopeless at climbing. I keep getting dropped." He asked me what kind of training I was doing and I said I was doing about 100-120 kilometre rides. Then I said: "Look, tell me straight, do you think I have what it takes to become a cyclist or not?" Next thing I know he's got hold of my arms and he's rubbing them up and down, pressing on them. He didn't touch my legs, just my arms and my neck. Then he says: "You can become a cyclist, no question. Your big problem is that you're not doing it right. You have to do more climbing when you train. Go away and try that, and then write to me and let me know how you get on..." And he was right! I won 15 races the following season, and turned professional in 1958.

I was an independent but I rode for Ghigi-Coppi. The DS was a bloke called Quaglia but nobody could figure out what he was for because he didn't direct anything at all. It didn't matter though because I won six races, and the Italian Independents Championship. That wasn't bad for starters, and apparently I showed a lot of promise.

I trained with Coppi and the Bianchi lot. He wasn't winning any more but it was brutal all the same. You'd set off at about 9am and you'd be getting back in the dark. He was an unbelievable trainer but in the races he was stuffed; he was being pushed by people who weren't fit to tie his bootlaces. He still had the passion, but not the legs.

I remember the Tour of Lombardy. I got the train up to Milan and went for a ride. When we got back there was still no sign of

Coppi – he hadn't turned up. He finally arrived at 9am, covered in muck, his eyes as red as a beetroot. It was only about 120 kilometres from Novi but it was a filthy, horrible night, and we had Lombardy the following morning.

To be honest I can't say I knew him because he never spoke. If someone asked him something he'd answer but he was pretty monosyllabic. He wasn't ignorant, not at all, but he just didn't say anything. He just stayed in his room, in the dark, wearing dark sunglasses. I only roomed with him once but I'm reasonably certain he didn't say a word. It was a bit unnerving to be honest and I have not the faintest idea how he ever managed to have a relationship with that woman...

Anyway in 1959 I signed with EMI, Charly Gaul's team. We went to the first training camp on the Riviera and I don't think I saw Gaul. He'd go to the discotheque, go with women, whatever, but what he didn't do was train. I rode with him for two seasons and we never once trained together, not once. It was an Italian team and us Italian riders were there wanting to help him. You couldn't though because as far as he was concerned we were no use to him whatsoever. There were two other blokes from Luxembourg in the 'team' and they didn't even talk to us. When we rode the Giro they'd have breakfast in their rooms and they wouldn't even come down to dinner!

Gaul won the Giro. Don't ask me how because I still don't have the faintest idea how anybody could do that with the amount of training he did. Learco Guerra was DS and everybody talked about what a genius he was. That was nonsense as well because he was already suffering from Alzheimer's.

I stopped because being a professional cyclist was rubbish. I can't tell you precisely what went wrong, just that you never seemed to know whether you were coming or going...

——

Paolo Guazzini looked set for a glittering career when he won six races in 1958, his first professional season. Thereafter he spent three fruitless years riding on the same team as Charly Gaul, the great Luxembourgish Tour and Giro winner. Guazzini retired in 1962, aged 27. Fifty years on he's still doing 100 kilometre rides, and his route includes a 30 kilometre climb.

"Cavanna was already blind but he was Coppi's masseur and apparently he was an expert on young cyclists. People said he was some kind of Svengali…"

"I trained with Coppi and the Bianchi lot. He wasn't winning any more, but it was brutal all the same. He was an unbelievable trainer, but in the races he was stuffed; he was being pushed by people who weren't fit to tie his bootlaces. He still had the passion, but not the legs…"

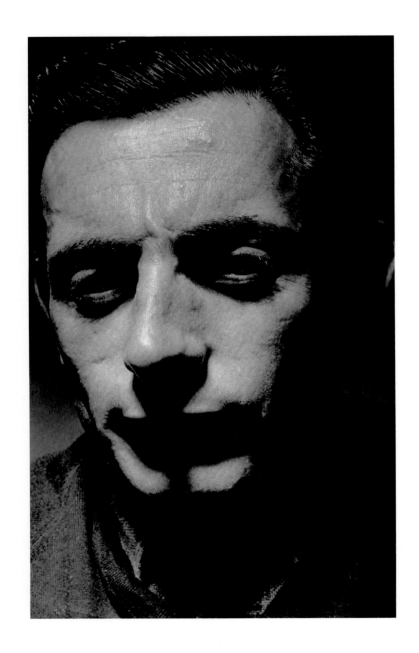

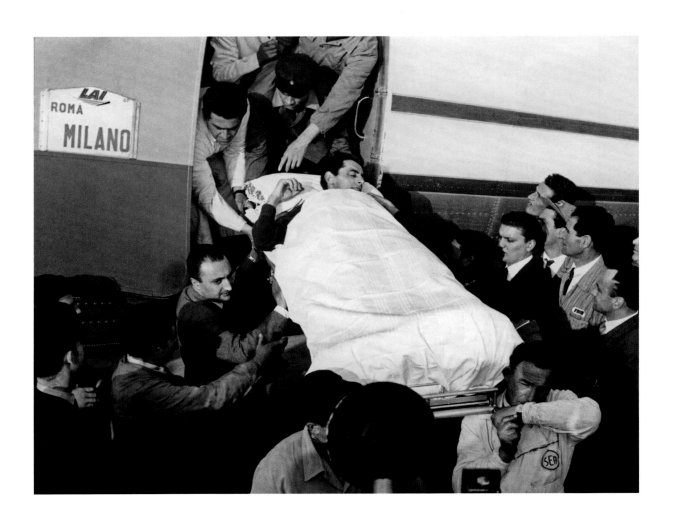

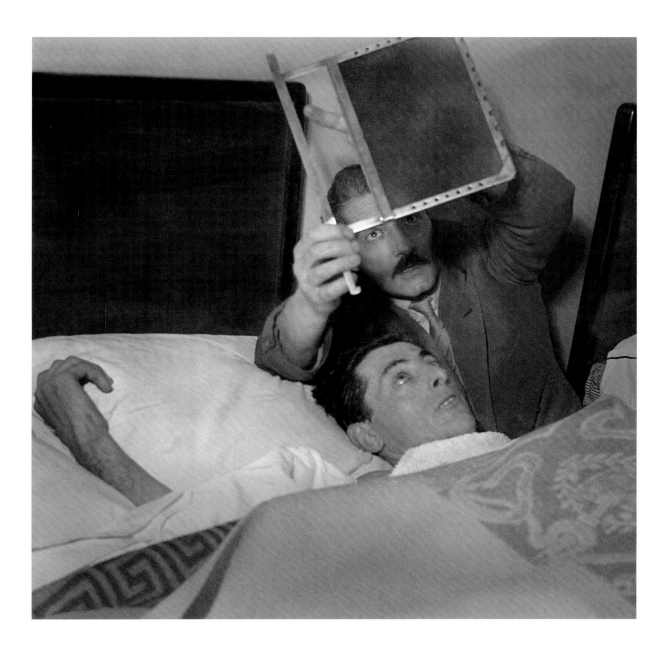

WALTER ALMAVIVA

b Vignole Borbera, 1933
pro 1958–1961

Runner up 1959 Giro dell'Appennino
Fifth 1960 Giro dell'Appennino
21st 1959 Giro di Lombardia

Pictured second left © Original author

Everyone round here was into cycling. There was always a great tradition but basically it was all about Coppi. When you grew up ten kilometres from Novi Ligure, as I did, it was almost part of your birthright. He was the king around here, no more and no less. He was the king, and this was his kingdom.

I started riding at 16, almost as a joke. There were a few kids round here who had these fancy racing bikes. I went out with them one day just on a normal bike and I dropped them on the climb. That was how it happened.

So now I'm out training and obviously you're running into them all the time. Fausto, Carrea, Milano, Gismondi; all the Bianchi lot. That was the beginning and eventually I plucked up the courage to talk to them. They saw that I was a decent rider and slowly Fausto and I became friends. I rode for him later, but fundamentally we were friends, do you understand?

I did military service like everyone else but because I was good at it I was basically free to ride. So in a practical sense I was a professional cyclist for those 18 months. In November 1954 there was a track meet at Rome, with Fausto and Gismondi. A friend and I went to watch, and I had Fausto sign an autograph for my commander. The following morning I got an order saying I had to go to the guardroom and Fausto was there waiting for me. He said to the boss of my section: "Keep an eye on this Almaviva for me. When he finishes here I want him in my team." Can you believe that? Fausto Coppi came to find *me*. Heaven knows what it was he thought he'd seen.

When I came back I started winning, nine races that year. We did Milan-Castellania, the Serse Coppi Memorial. I remember Tragella, the Bianchi DS, making a gesture to me. He was saying: "You know that if you win this you're in?" I won but then Tragella died and Fausto went to Carpano-Coppi.

I was supposed to turn professional in 1957 but I had an offer to stay amateur for the same salary. It was a team from Savigliano and they were offering me 50,000 lire a month, standard first year pro salary. A factory worker would have been earning about 40,000 but they were also offering me a 20,000 lire win bonus and 10,000 for second. Effectively I had a choice to make. If I signed for a professional team with a leader who won I would have done well out of it, but if I didn't I'd have been earning pretty ordinary money. There was the prestige of being a professional - albeit a *gregario*, obviously - or a good chance to make decent money by staying another year as an amateur.

The next year Girardengo offered me a two-year contract with his professional team. I went to Alessandria to sign it but when I got home Fausto was waiting for me with the *Dama Bianca*. I said: "But why didn't you ask me sooner? I've just signed for Girardengo!" He said: "Well I didn't want you to feel obliged to sign for me." I said: "Well I didn't feel obliged because I thought you didn't want me!" So anyway I rode the Giro for Girardengo but then the team went bust in the February. It was too late to get another contract but Fausto saw to it that I rode and got paid.

I knew the *Dama* well and I also know that most of what is said about her is rubbish. I would say that she was possessive but that it was her who made 'The Fausto' a *signor*. He changed in the way he dressed, yes, but he also changed as a man when he was with her. He came from farming stock and Bruna had always wanted him to stay that way. When Serse had died she'd wanted him to stop but Fausto couldn't stop. How could he stop? What was he supposed to do?

The *Dama Bianca* demanded respect from the people around her, and courtesy. But she was calm and she let him get on with his career. I can't say I spent a lot of time with her because I was always out riding with Fausto but when I saw her I got on fine with her, no problem at all. A lot of people had issues with her but at the end of the day it was his life and he decided. It had nothing to do with anybody else and for people to take issue with her was ridiculous. Fausto wasn't their property and they had no right to make judgements about her when they didn't know her.

Obviously I was much younger but Bruna hadn't wanted anything to do with us, or with cycling. When you went round there Fausto's mum would give you dried fruit and stuff, but you never saw Bruna.

So I can't say that he was unhappy at home with the *Dama*, and that he carried on riding just to get out of the house. I always thought that he continued to ride simply because he was in love with his bike, and in love with being out on it...

The *Dama* didn't want him to go to Africa, it's true, but that's because it was Christmas and she wanted him home with Faustino.

The truth is that when he was dying he was pleading to see his daughter Marina, but Bruna didn't take her. He saw Faustino, and Giulia was there right to the end. I was there till the end as well. I was there the morning he died. Right till the end...

——

Walter Almaviva rode professionally for four years. Upon the death of his idol he signed for *Il Campionissimo's* old team, Bianchi. He still lives in Vignole Borbera, less than half an hour's bike ride from Coppi's Novi Ligure.

"It was her who made 'The Fausto' a *signor*. He changed in the way he dressed, yes, but he also changed as a man when he was with her..."

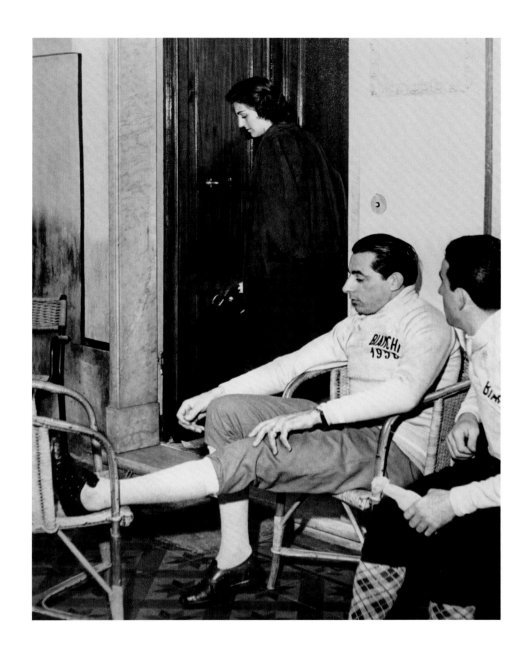

RAPHAEL GEMINIANI

b Clermont-Ferrand, 1925
pro 1946–1960

Stage winner, King of the Mountains and second overall
1951 Tour de France
Winner of seven Tour de France stages
French national champion 1953
Fourth 1955 Giro d'Italia

© Offside/L'Équipe

The idea was that all the most important French riders would be going. That meant me, Anglade, Anquetil, Rivière, Hassenforder and Bobet. A few days before we were due to fly Bobet called me and said he was ill and couldn't come. Obviously it was in the papers and so Fausto must have heard about it.

He called me and asked if he could come. He loved hunting and so the idea of a trip to Africa really appealed to him. He wasn't bothered about what he'd be getting paid.

We did an exhibition ride on the Sunday, 100 kilometres out and back with a few of the locals. The following day they flew us to Fada N'gourma. We were taken to a villa owned an Italian businessman, and he organised a big party for us. Only one of the bungalows had anti-mosquito netting and because Anquetil was there with Janine, his wife, it was decided that they would have that one. Fausto and I shared, and it was a pretty miserable night. It was as hot as hell and the mosquitos were everywhere. Fausto seemed to be having an awful time. I shouted to him: "Fausto, put your head under the blanket like I have! That way they won't get you, and you'll get some sleep!" but he said *Porca miseria*, Gem, they're eating me alive!"

We did the hunt, and Fausto spoke about a contract he was going to sign with a new French team. They were going to use his frames, and he was excited it meant the bikes would get exposure in France as well. He'd signed to ride one last season for San Pellegrino, with Bartali as DS. He was looking forward to that because he'd discovered Romeo Venturelli and he was convinced he could help him to become a champion.

We flew back into Paris and we went our separate ways. I rang him on 19 December and told him I wasn't feeling great; that I thought I had the flu. He said he wasn't feeling too well either and his symptoms were the same. He said he felt a bit tired, short of energy. We both said we'd take it easy over Christmas and thought nothing more of it.

I had a normal Christmas with the family but then on Boxing Day evening I woke up feeling really ill. I had an unquenchable thirst but when I got out of bed to drink something I collapsed. I started throwing up and I was freezing and sweating at the same time. I didn't know what was wrong with me but I knew it was something bigger than flu. I had a temperature of 40 degrees and no matter what they did I wasn't getting any better. When the newspapers reported it we had a call from a doctor specialising in tropical diseases. He suggested it could be malaria, and so my brother rushed my blood to the Pasteur Institute in Paris. The following day they called and confirmed it. They cured me with a simple quinine injection...

—

Raphaël Géminiani contracted malaria in Burkina Faso but was saved at the eleventh hour. So too was Adriano Laiolo, a 21-year-old hunting enthusiast who had travelled with Coppi. He survived because the nurse treating him had recently returned from Africa and recognised the symptoms.

"Because Anquetil was there with Janine, his wife, it was decided that they would have the only mosquito net. Fausto and I shared, and it was a pretty miserable night. It was as hot as hell and the mosquitos were everywhere..."

PHOTOGRAPHY CREDITS

Cover
Fausto Coppi, star attraction
© *Foto Agenzia Omega Fotocronache*
Milano di Vito Liverani

Page 12
Punzonatura. Giro d'Italia, 1952
© *Publifoto/Olycom*

Page 14
Giro di Lombardia, 1947.
Bartali was runner up, at 5'24"
© *Publifoto/Olycom*

Page 15
Lombardia 1947
© *Publifoto/Olycom*

Page 16
Splendid isolation. Giro di Campania
© *Foto Agenzia Omega Fotocronache*
Milano di Vito Liverani

Page 18
Collarbone. Again
© *Publifoto/Olycom*

Page 19
Into the arena
© *Publifoto/Olycom*

Page 20
In fuga. Bartali clings on...
© *Foto Agenzia Omega Fotocronache*
Milano di Vito Liverani

Page 22
Giro
© *Offside/L'Équipe*

Page 23
Fausto's curse
© *Foto Agenzia Omega Fotocronache*
Milano di Vito Liverani

Page 24
VIP treatment
© *Foto Agenzia Omega Fotocronache*
Milano di Vito Liverani

Page 26
Giving them Hell. Floating at
Paris-Roubaix, 1950
© *Offside/L'Équipe*

Page 27
Leading and winning the
1950 Paris-Roubaix
© *Offside/L'Équipe*

Page 28
Runner up Maurice Diot said:
"I won Paris-Roubaix! Coppi was
riding a different race to the rest..."
© *Offside/L'Équipe*

Page 30
Public property
© *Publifoto/Olycom*

Page 35
In the south
© *Publifoto/Olycom*

Page 36
Rinascimento. Italy rolls
up its sleeves...
© *Foto Agenzia Omega Fotocronache*
Milano di Vito Liverani

Page 38
The great unwashed.
Giro d'Italia, 1947
© *Foto Agenzia Omega Fotocronache*
Milano di Vito Liverani

Page 40
At Varigotti
© *Foto Agenzia Omega Fotocronache*
Milano di Vito Liverani

Page 42
From the ground up. Luigi
Malabrocca, the *maglia nera*
© *Foto Agenzia Omega Fotocronache*
Milano di Vito Liverani

Pages 44–47
Partenza
© *Foto Agenzia Omega Fotocronache*
Milano di Vito Liverani

Page 48
"Un uomo solo è al comando"
© Foto Agenzia Omega Fotocronache
Milano di Vito Liverani

Page 53
With a young Jacques Anquetil
© Publifoto/Olycom

Page 54
Fixed
© Publifoto/Olycom

Page 56
48 × 20
© Publifoto/Olycom

Page 57
Please keep off the grass
© Olympya/Olycom

Page 58
Tubolari
© Foto Agenzia Omega Fotocronache
Milano di Vito Liverani

Page 59
Godless
© Publifoto/Olycom

Page 60
Blessed
© Foto Agenzia Omega Fotocronache
Milano di Vito Liverani

Page 65
Young and old, rich and poor...
© Olympya/Olycom

Page 66
"They didn't stand a chance..."
© Publifoto/Olycom

Page 68
Clean jersey, goggles, fresh bartape.
Champion of the world
© Olympya/Olycom

Page 69
Righteous among the nations, 1954
© Foto Agenzia Omega Fotocronache
Milano di Vito Liverani

Page 70
1952 Tour de France victory
lap at the Parc des Princes
© Offside/L'Équipe

Page 71
With Hugo Koblet, stage six,
1954 Giro
© Foto Agenzia Omega Fotocronache
Milano di Vito Liverani

Page 72
Palermo, before the storm
© Publifoto/Olycom

Page 73
Campionissimo
© Publifoto/Olycom

Page 76
Rome. An audience
with Gino Bartali
© Foto Agenzia Omega Fotocronache
Milano di Vito Liverani

Page 78
Il Musichiere, 1959
© Publifoto/Olycom

Page 79
Playing the game
© Publifoto/Olycom

Page 80
Détente. The Corrieri effect
© Foto Agenzia Omega Fotocronache
Milano di Vito Liverani

Page 85
Full gas. With Bartali, 1948 Giro
© Foto Agenzia Omega Fotocronache
Milano di Vito Liverani

Page 195
Under seige
© *Olympya/Olycom*

Pages 196–197
Nothing can stop us now
© *Foto Agenzia Omega Fotocronache
Milano di Vito Liverani*

Pages 198–199
In public. Absolutely fearless
© *Publifoto/Olycom*

Page 203
Desperately missing Marina
© *Olympya/Olycom*

Page 204
Money for old rope in a packed
Vigorelli velodrome
© *Olympya/Olycom*

Page 205
Big star, big bikes
© *Olympya/Olycom*

Page 206
Track racing was big business
and Coppi knew it
© *Foto Agenzia Omega Fotocronache
Milano di Vito Liverani*

Page 208
Lap one; Messina already
has two metres
© *Original author*

Page 209
At the Vigorelli again
© *Olympya/Olycom*

Page 210
What is he if not a cyclist?
What else can he do?
© *Foto Agenzia Omega Fotocronache
Milano di Vito Liverani*

Page 215
Shelter
© *Foto Agenzia Omega Fotocronache
Milano di Vito Liverani*

Page 216
The laying on of hands
© *Foto Agenzia Omega Fotocronache
Milano di Vito Liverani*

Pages 218
Twentieth century religious festival,
southern Italy
© *Publifoto/Olycom*

Page 220–221
With Bobet and Gismondi
© *Olympya/Olycom*

Page 222
Piazza San Carlo
© *Publifoto/Olycom*

Page 223
Millions and millions of Italians
© *Publifoto/Olycom*

Page 224
Papal State
© *Publifoto/Olycom*

Page 226
Heavy
© *Publifoto/Olycom*

Pages 228–229
These people have homes to go to
© *Publifoto/Olycom*

Page 233
Rocket fuel. Giro, 1952
© *Foto Agenzia Omega Fotocronache
Milano di Vito Liverani*

Pages 234–239
The rubber factory
© *Publifoto/Olycom*

Page 240
A quiver of Specialismas
© *Publifoto/Olycom*

Page 254
1957, with Alfredo Binda
and Nino Defilippis
© *Olympya/Olycom*

Page 263
No matter who they are, a racer
always pins on their own number
© *Olympya/Olycom*

Page 241
Heart as big as a bucket. With kids
crippled in the bombings
© *Publifoto/Olycom*

Page 255
With Defilippis; the past and
the present of Italian cycling
© *Original author*

Pages 264 – 265
Trapped
© *Olympya/Olycom*

Page 242
Epicentre
© *Publifoto/Olycom*

Pages 256 – 257
The Grand Prix des Nations
© *Publifoto/Olycom*

Page 266
Still hounded
© *Foto Agenzia Omega Fotocronache
Milano di Vito Liverani*

Pages 244 – 245
With Ettore Milano. All is good
© *Olympya/Olycom*

Page 258
Learning to crawl
© *Foto Agenzia Omega Fotocronache
Milano di Vito Liverani*

Page 267
1957. The dying of the light
© *Foto Agenzia Omega Fotocronache
Milano di Vito Liverani*

Page 250
With Mario Fossati,
the great journalist
© *Foto Agenzia Omega Fotocronache
Milano di Vito Liverani*

Page 260
24th
© *Olympya/Olycom*

Page 271
Sanctuary, with Biagio Cavanna
© *Publifoto/Olycom*

Page 251
With Louison Bobet and
the gentlemen of the press
© *Olympya/Olycom*

Page 261
2nd
© *Olympya/Olycom*

Page 272
Pictures from a museum
© *Olympya/Olycom*

Page 252
Inexplicably, we find
ourselves drinking tea...
© *Publifoto/Olycom*

Page 262
Neither one thing nor the other.
With Mario Gervasini, Pietro
Nascimbene and Angelo Coletto
© *Publifoto/Olycom*

Page 273
Il ceccho. The blind ex-boxer
with the magic hands
© *Foto Agenzia Omega Fotocronache
Milano di Vito Liverani*

THANKS

This book was born in the offices of Italian picture agency Olycom in Milan, 2009. There we sat, in between bulging filing cabinets, sifting through piles of tatty prints, glass slides and gelatine negatives – the dusty and scratched spoils from 100 years of Italian cycle racing history. Herbie's book Maglia Rosa – Triumph and Tragedy at the Giro d'Italia was all the better for these many hours of painstaking print shuffling. During this search we realised how powerful the collection of images of Fausto Coppi was. It's hard to know why: perhaps he just had a character that appealed to the photographers. But he was never just a face in the crowd. In every one he is unmistakably Coppi and undeniably cool. The hit rate of photographic gems was exceptional and the hours turned into days as we were sidetracked by hundreds of beautiful prints.

Regular Rouleur magazine contributor Taz Darling was with us on that first trip to Milan and it was her enthusiasm for these stacks of images – as a photographer rather than a fan – that started the Coppi project rolling. Herbie was pretty ambivalent about writing a biography of Coppi per se, but the strength of the imagery meant the Italian stuck in all our minds. Keen for an original approach, Herbie travelled the length and breadth of Italy in search of the men who rode alongside Il Campionissimo. Their stories are told here.

The next time we headed to Milan, we spread the Coppi net a bit further afield, leading to Vito Liverani's archive at Omega. Vito was taking pictures when Coppi was racing and is one of Italian cycling's most prolific photojournalists. Two days surrounded by Vito and his negatives provided even more content. Olycom's library was raided once more for additional exclusive and rarely seen images, and Offside / L'Équipe provided some French flavour from the Tour de France, Grand Prix des Nations and Paris-Roubaix.

Our heartfelt thanks go to the image experts at these agencies, notably Daniela Mericio, Anna Locatelli and Maurizio Scotti at Olycom and David Wilkinson from Offside / L'Équipe. Also to Vito Liverani, Denise Nani and Fabrizio Zambelli from Foto Agenzia Omega Fotocronache Milano di Vito Liverani. Closer to home, many thanks to Charlotte Croft and Nick Ascroft at Bloomsbury, and to Rouleur's publisher Bruce Sandell, who all saw the value of this project, even as a sketched idea, and showed great patience as we limped towards the deadline. Thanks to all the contributors, especially to the designer Rob Johnston and to the book's sub editor Claire Read, also to Linda Duong, Edwin Ingram, Ian Cleverly and everyone in the Rouleur offices.

The contents of this book are, intentionally, a mixture of chronology, social documentary and personal account. With no small measure of photographic genius, it's impossible to tell who shot exactly what, or in some cases even when, but it's some of the best work of the era and we are deeply indebted to Nick Giordano, Mario Germoglio, Luca Silano and Walfrido Chiarini, Pippo Terreni, Evaristo Fusar, Raul Fornezza, Carlo Fumagalli, Tino Petrelli, Enrico Belluschi and Carlo Martini.
Guy Andrews

Author's thanks to Antonio Ronconi, for his kindness at a time of great personal loss. Marco Trasmondi, for his generosity of spirit, and for helping me to decipher Tuscan dialect. Pino Favero, for being Pino Favero. Overwhelming thanks to all the riders. They were, without exception, a joy.
Herbie Sykes

Herbie Sykes is a cycling historian and the author of two previous books about the Giro d'Italia: Maglia Rosa was published by Rouleur to enormous acclaim in 2011, while Cycling Weekly described The Eagle of the Canavese as 'a gem of a book'. Sykes lives in Turin and is a regular contributor to Rouleur magazine.

Rouleur is the highly acclaimed cycling magazine, issued eight times a year. It brings together leading cycling writers and photographers to convey the essence and imagery of road racing. Rouleur features photography and serious writing celebrating the passion and beauty of the sport and has built a dedicated following among both cycling fans and the most influential bike riders in the world.

www.rouleur.cc

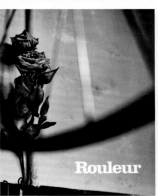

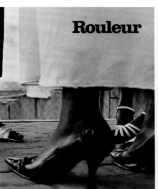

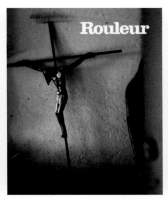

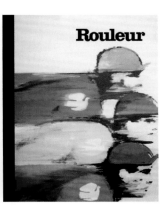

Books available from Rouleur

Maglia Rosa – Triumph and Tragedy at the Giro d'Italia

The Rouleur Annual Volume 5

Le Métier – The Seasons of a Professional Cyclist

Angelo Fausto Coppi
15 September 1919 — 2 January 1960

Five Giri with 22 stage wins, two Tours with nine stage wins, the hour record, the World Championship, five Giri di Lombardia, three Milan-Sanremo, four national road titles, two Grand Prix des Nations, Paris-Roubaix, Flèche Wallone... Fausto Coppi's *palmares*, though extraordinary in the context of post-war bike racing, is in some respects illusory. If Eddy Merckx was the best cyclist who ever lived, Coppi was irrefutably the greatest. That greatness could never be measured in a list. Rather it is to be found in the profound effect he, his genius and the vicissitudes of his life had on ordinary Italians, and on a continent of sports fans.